Read this book!

RICK LAW AND ZACH HESSELBAUM CAN HELP YOU TO AVOID THE POTHOLES AND ENJOY THE RIDE

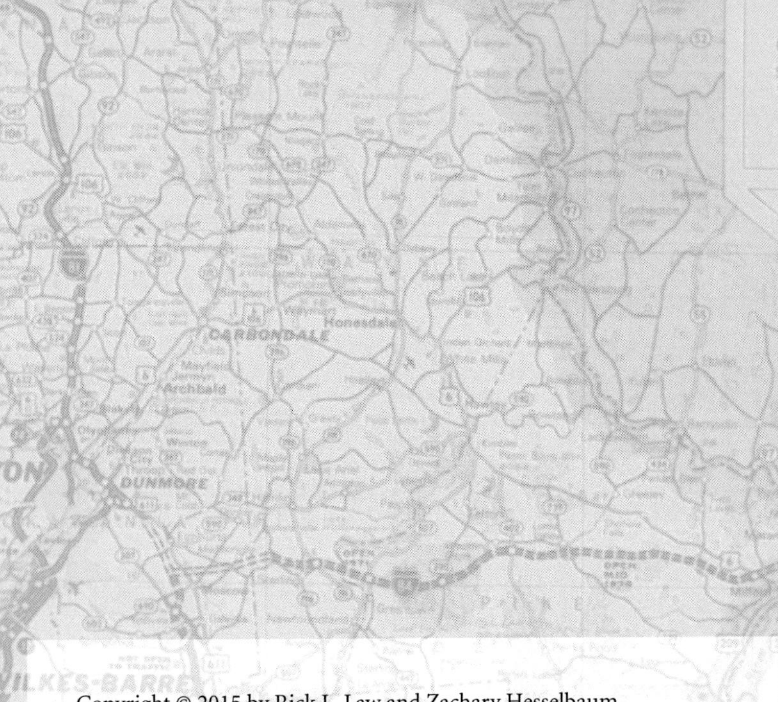

Printed in the United States of America.

ISBN: 978-1-63385-056-9

Designed and published by

Word Association Publishers
205 Fifth Avenue
Tarentum, Pennsylvania 15084
www.wordassociation.com
1.800.827.7903

Avoiding the Potholes

Cruising THROUGH RETIREMENT

second edition

A ROAD MAP TO PROTECT YOU FROM WALL $TREET GAMES, RUINOUS HEALTHCARE COSTS AND A GOVERNMENT GONE WILD!

RICK L. LAW, J.D.

ZACHARY HESSELBAUM, J.D., LL.M. TAXATION

Local Mileage
Interstate
State
SCALE OF MILES
CARBONDALE
Honesdale
Archbald
Mayfield
DUNMORE
WILKES-BARRE
PIKE
Milford
Skytop
Newton
Jim Thorpe
Lehighton
Palmerton
Bangor
Hackettstown
Washington
Hampton
Nazareth
EASTON
Northampton
PHILLIPSBURG
Wilson
Fountain Hill
Hellertown
BETHLEHEM
ALLENTOWN

Contents

Meet the Authors **1**

Introduction **5**

1. The Income Crisis
Yesterday's investment rules don't apply in
today's retirement landscape. 13

2. Longevity Risk
How to plan for a very long life 27

3. A Whole New Angle on Long-Term Care
Options for funding your future
health needs. 53

4. Medicare: The Dollars and Cents
What you need to know about Medicare so
you won't lose your home 77

5. A Weekend Away
A children's story to simply explain estate
planning with trusts 103

6. The Law Elderlaw Pyramid of Estate and Asset Protection Planning
A level-by-level approach to planning 147

7. Asset Protection Tools for Business (Pyramid of Protection Level 6)
Don't lose the family farm!. 169

8. Social Security and Retirement Income
What women really need to know about
their future funds. 189

9. Avoiding the Common Potholes
From unexpected care expenses to remarriage to gifting 215

10. The Elder Care Journey
Dealing with declining health, increasing expenses, and the need for more medical care 257

11. How to Find a Trusted Advisor
Tips to identify the top 5 percent of professionals . . 293

Epilogue
Keith and Diane's Story. 305

Appendix 1
Michael Lewis Bio, Contributor to Chapter 4 309

Appendix 2
Rick's "Keepers": A Bibliography of Books on Investing 311

Appendix 3
Professional Memberships 315

Appendix 4
What Clients and Their Families Say about Us 317

Index 323

Meet the Authors

Rick L. Law, J.D., is the founder and lead attorney of Law ElderLaw, LLP and Estate Planning Center. The law firm is dedicated to advocating for individuals who seek guidance to make wise decisions about life, death, and protecting those they love. Most of the law firm's clients are seniors. Over the years, the firm has become renowned in its retirement, estate, asset protection, and elder law solutions. The law firm takes a holistic view by not only dealing with planning for retirement but also protecting the surviving spouse after the first death. According to the magazine *Leading Lawyers*, other attorneys in Illinois have consistently ranked Rick Law as the leading elder law estate planning attorney in Illinois. Rick likes to say that Law ElderLaw serves seniors and those who love them.

Rick received his Juris Doctor of Laws from Northern Illinois University College of Law. He focuses his practice on elder law, retirement, taxation, estate protection, nursing home Medicaid, and Veterans Administration benefits. He is a member of a number of national organizations, including the National Academy of Elder Law Attorneys, Leading Lawyer Network, Wealth Counsel, and the National Organization of Veterans' Advocates. He is also a frequent public speaker and an author. In 2013, the American Bar Association published a book entitled *Alzheimer's and the Law: Counseling Clients with Dementia and Their Families*, by Rick Law and Kerry Peck.

When he is not writing, teaching, or serving seniors, Rick is a fan of all things "cowboy." Being raised in the 1950's, Rick loves everything about horses and cinema and TV cowboys. His favorite western stars of old are Hopalong Cassidy, Roy Rogers, and Zorro, who have inspired his love of horses and the Old West. During the last 30 years, Rick has taken at least one progressive horseback ride per year in the West. He lives in Oswego, Illinois, which is his hometown. He and his wife Rosemary have four children: Adam, Diana, Catherine, and Ethan. Both he and Rose delight in their four grandchildren: Lucy, Daphne, Evan, and Phoebe.

Zachary J. Hesselbaum, J.D., LL.M. Taxation, is a partner of Law ElderLaw, LLP and Estate Planning Center. Zach specifically focuses his practice in the areas of estate and tax planning, elder law, asset protection, veterans benefits, and Illinois Medicaid. This focus allows for holistic planning that provides successful solutions for retirement issues, asset protection, and elder law matters. Zach has been a featured presenter for the Illinois Institute of Continuing Legal Education on the topic of veterans benefits. In addition, he has had articles published on elder law topics by the Illinois State Bar Journal, Kane County Bar Journal, and DuPage County Bar Briefs. Zach received both his undergraduate degree and his Juris Doctor from Valparaiso University in Indiana. In 2013, Zach obtained his Masters of Law in Taxation from DePaul University College of Law in Chicago.

Zach is originally from Oswego, Illinois, and currently lives in Naperville, Illinois, with his wife Kelly and his son Rockne. Zach enjoys all things sports-related and can often be seen with his family cheering on the Chicago White Sox or searching for memorabilia to add to his collection.

Introduction

We can all learn from our mistakes, but I have found that it is a lot wiser and less painful to learn from the mistakes of others. When clients come to see us, they want us to be their trustworthy guides throughout the retirement and elder care journey. We see over 500 client families per year, so we have learned a lot from trying to help to correct other people's mistakes. We can help our clients avoid many of the common potholes along the retirement and elder care journey.

There is only one old lawyer at our law firm—me. It's good to have at least one old lawyer at Law ElderLaw, but it's even better to have many fine, capable, young lawyers who will be able to serve our clients and their families over the decades ahead.

The majority of our over 500 annual clients are couples who are still in the healthy, vigorous portion of aging. Many of our clients are widows or widowers who have already lost a precious spouse. Over the last ten years, Law ElderLaw has continued to serve younger and younger clients. When the law firm began in 2004, the primary focus was on those who already had an unwelcome diagnosis such as Alzheimer's or Parkinson's disease. Now, we commonly see clients who are in their 50s and many, many clients in their early 60s. We still see lots of people who have received bad news from their doctors. It is our job to serve our clients, to help them to make wise decisions about life, death, and protecting those they love.

There is a distinctive difference between being an estate planner and what we do for our clients. Since 2004, we have focused on giving advice not only about estate planning, but also about how to survive and thrive during the aging process. To do that, we need to understand a wide variety of issues that face our clients. We need to understand how healthcare will be provided for them and how healthcare is paid for. In addition, we need to help our clients understand that, if done correctly, their estate plan can have profound, positive benefits for them while they are still alive. Their estate plan should be designed with their survivor spouse and loved ones in mind. How their estate plan is done, funded, and financed can make an enormous difference in the quality of our clients' lives and those they leave behind. We feel very fortunate because there are few attorneys and/or senior advisors who have had the opportunity to learn firsthand from the financial and legal decisions and mistakes of over 5,000 lifetimes of past-client decision makers.

As you read this book, we hope that two light bulbs will go on for you. The first light bulb is that estate planning can be far more than the typical estate plan, and it can provide benefits far beyond what you've dreamed of. If you are typical, then you've had very little education in the area of estate planning, and your view of estate planning is most likely very straightforward. You may think, "If I die, everything goes to my sweetheart. And if my sweetheart is gone, then divide up everything equally and put it into my children's checking accounts." That may be all that you need, but every month, we are employed by clients just like you who seek solutions that provide greater benefits for themselves, their survivor spouse, and their survivor children than what that typical view of estate planning would provide. It's our job to teach you how to benefit from those solutions.

The second light bulb is this: we want to help you understand what I call the elder care journey. Most people do not understand Medicare, Social Security, nursing home Medicaid, and veterans benefits. If you don't understand those things, you are still a normal, capable adult. It's not your job to understand those things. In fact, it's not the job of most attorneys to understand those things. We, as elder law estate planners, have to know about those things so we can make sure that our clients are never out of money and never out of options while they are alive. And while we cannot guarantee that you'll never be out of money or out of options, our goal is to make sure that you are able to maximize your opportunities with the resources you have, not only financially, but with governmental benefits and with your family.

In this book, Zach Hesselbaum, J.D., L.L.M. Taxation, and I join forces to share with you how to find the best place to stand in today's economic and technological earthquake. We know that most of our clients are looking for certain things from a legal and/or financial advisor:

1. Safety, because it's too hard to get back what you have lost. Safety comes in a lot of forms and there is nothing that doesn't have a downside to it. Our clients want to know both the risk and the reward of proposed solutions.

2. A reasonable rate of return on your money. Most people do not expect to be stock market wizards. And they want to save in a consistent way to be able to support their lifestyle. It's important to understand that the rules that helped you to accumulate your assets are not the same rules that will dictate how best to use what you've accumulated. It is far more complex to plan for and to implement appropriate retirement asset distribution strategies than it ever was to accumulate the money in the first place.

3. Simplicity, because nobody enjoys feeling like a fool. Everybody wants to make legal and financial decisions that they can understand. We strive to be counselors who make sure you can understand what we're proposing and why.

4. Income for life. Nobody wants to run out of money before they die. If you're out of money, you're out of options. The decisions that you make—ranging from Social Security to IRAs to asset protection—will make the difference between a healthy, vigorous retirement and one of impoverishment. Zach and I know that many retirees make lots of poor investment and legal choices that are unsafe, complex, and with pie-in-the-sky promises.

Years ago, as a young tax attorney, I would look at many proposals being given to my clients and I would ask myself this question, "What in the world is the motivation for the creation and sale of this to my client?" I would review the documents and look at the enormous risk and the extraordinary promises of great returns and I would say to myself, "Why does my client want to do this? Why does their advisor want to sell this?" Eventually, I came to create an acronym that I call "YTB": Yield to Broker. Ever since those early days as a tax lawyer, I have asked myself in every financial transaction to make sure I understand what the yield is to the broker. How much money is he or she making on this proposed product or deal? You need to know not only what you're supposedly going to be earning from a proposed investment, but also how much your broker is making to sell it to you.

Zach Hesselbaum is a great guy! I once wrote an article to go into two local Bar Association journals and the title was "Everybody Loves Zach." Zach has a master's degree in Tax Law and he has the experience of working with several thousand families. He has become the Head of our Estate Planning and Asset Protection Department.

I am Rick Law. I am an addict of lifelong learning and a somewhat cynical 64-year-old attorney. Over the years, I have read and collected (at last count) over 120 books on investing. I have taken numerous courses, and I continue to take courses, on how best to advise clients and their financial advisors. I am honored to have been chosen by other attorneys as the "Top Elder Law Estate Planner in Illinois" according to a survey by *Leading Lawyer Magazine.* In addition, one of the highlights of my professional career has been co-authoring the book *Alzheimer's and the Law: Counseling Clients with Dementia and Their Families,* published by the American Bar Association.

At this point in my life, I look forward to being able to serve my clients as long as I continue to be both physically and mentally able. But it is a great joy for me to know that I'm working with Zach Hesselbaum and my daughter, Diana M. Law, as my law partners. As we present you this book, our voices will be blended together into a common "we." It is my sincere desire that you will be benefited by this book. If you take to heart the two light bulbs that I mentioned earlier, then you will make better decisions both for you and your survivor spouse.

So, if you want to sleep better, read this book! It was written by two lawyers who work together to provide boomer retirees, maturing seniors, and frail elders with holistic legal and financial solutions.

Rick L. Law

Chapter 1

THE INCOME CRISIS

YESTERDAY'S INVESTMENT RULES DON'T APPLY IN TODAY'S RETIREMENT LANDSCAPE

We all want safety (the return of our principal) and protection from inflation (earning more than enough to compensate for the loss in value of our dollars), especially as we're in our retirement years. This book offers helpful, hopeful, and useful ideas you can choose today that will make your retirement ride more comfortable.

The U.S. Government and the Federal Reserve have created a zero-interest-rate world. Their goal is to force prudent investors into higher risk investments and make financing less expensive for the government and for banks.

The front cover of the book shows how we all want to feel as we cruise through retirement, and the very first page shows how most retirees feel—shell-shocked and immobilized by fear. To quote a client:

> *"We've got an income crisis. It wasn't supposed to be like this. We played by the rules. I thought we did everything right. I worked hard to save and invest so Betty and I would have enough to comfortably live off our income. But now we're spending our principal just to stay afloat. I don't know how this could have happened. They must have changed the rules."*

This man had a successful career as an administrative executive. He and his wife are both 67 years old. They're careful, frugal, and conservative. He's an analytical type who researched their investments and created a model diversified portfolio with a balance of stocks and bonds. It was all supposed to work to generate an average return of 11 percent per year, as based on long-term historical results. Had history repeated itself, that return would have been more than sufficient to fund their lifestyle and maintain their portfolio's principal value.

But their well-laid plans blew up! Their savings were devastated by the technology bubble meltdown, followed by a sideways stock market, the world financial system crash, and finally governmental policies that created zero-interest returns on safe investments.

The supposedly "right" answers about how to provide for a successful retirement just don't seem to work anymore. Senior investors are searching for the *new* right answers to protect their lifestyle. They don't have the luxury of looking back for the right answers—they're pioneers, a group of retirees like the world has never seen before.

Never in the history of human existence have millions of people had the *probability* of living to be more than 85 years of age. That's right—today the average life expectancy of the U.S. citizen has increased to 78.7 years, and millions of people will exceed that life expectancy by a decade or more.

When thinking about the joint life expectancy of a husband and wife, really old age becomes almost a certainty. The longevity statistics for a healthy couple, both age 65, indicate that at least one will live to be over 90 years of age. (And at least one will most likely spend two and a half to three years in a nursing home.)

Just to emphasize how fundamentally different the retiree universe is today, there are now *two full generations* of retirees alive: the baby boomers and their parents, the "greatest generation."

HOW THINGS HAVE CHANGED

We have seen the United States evolve from the world's greatest creditor nation to the biggest debtor nation in world history. Perhaps even more shocking to both baby boomers and their parents is that we now owe over $3.5 trillion dollars to the Chinese government. Who could have ever imagined that during our lifetimes the communist Chinese would be more fiscally prudent than the United States of America?

The work world has also changed drastically. Jobs in agriculture, construction, and manufacturing are declining, while work in government, healthcare, and business is on the rise. Today there are fewer than 12 million manufacturing jobs left in the United States, but there are 22.5 million government jobs—and growing.

We grew up in and benefited from the post-World War II era of prosperity that eventually fueled a massive stock market run-up. The stock market peaked in 2000 and took a nosedive that same year when the technology bubble burst. Since then, there have been some rallies in the market, but (after adjusting for inflation) its dollar value hasn't come close to what it was before.

It is true that at this particular moment in late 2014, the stock market has once again achieved a new high. In fact, empirically, financial advisors state that from the year 2000 to now that Fortune 500 company stocks have done an annualized gain of 11 percent. However, those same pundits have calculated that the average investor has only earned approximately 3.6 percent. Why the difference? For you to have realized the 11 percent per year gain, you would have had to tolerate the nauseating dives and avoided the urge to sell. Unfortunately, most of us who are normal human investors typically buy stocks at the wrong time and sell stocks at the wrong time. We have been further assaulted and insulted by how many times the stock market has risen and fallen within our recent memory. To a very high degree, senior investors are now frozen in their tracks, afraid to make a move forward.

"Dollar value" is another important concept. The world is awash in dollars that the U.S. Treasury has pumped out to deal with the financial market mess and the enormous amount of deficit spending by the U.S. government. In fiscal 2014, the U.S. government borrowed about 18 cents of every dollar it spent!

Inflation due to excess money supply has pummeled the finances of seniors on fixed incomes. The average cost of the daily essentials—food, for example—increases annually. *Money* magazine recently indicated that beef is up a shocking 56 percent just since 2010; eggs, butter, milk, and fresh produce are all also on the rise. In other words, buying the essentials requires more and more of a person's fixed income. Yet the U.S. government says it's worried about *deflation* pressures. That's because the government has its own way of measuring inflation, and the formula has been designed to underemphasize the things that most normal people buy.

The government uses a weighted formula for determining the Consumer Price Index (CPI), and according to that formula the government determined that the inflation during 2014 was 0.8 percent. You know from everyday experience that the actual costs of fuel and food and medicine are rising rapidly. But if your income is calibrated to the CPI—as are Social Security benefits—then your income crisis is just getting worse.

To combat the 2008 financial meltdown, the U.S. Treasury lent trillions of dollars at roughly 0 percent to big U.S. banks, big foreign banks and the "too big to fail" Wall Street brokerage/banking firms. In other words, the richest and most speculative groups in the world are receiving free money from the U.S. government, which they in turn are encouraged to lend. Unfortunately for Main Street America—which cannot get a loan—the favored borrower is the U.S. Treasury.

That's right! Our treasury is lending money at 0 percent to the "fat cats," and then borrowing it back from them at roughly 2.05 percent for a 10-year treasury bond. By the way, that's called an "infinite yield." If you have no cost of capital and you can get a return on lending or speculation with that money, the return on investment calculation is astronomical. No wonder the folks in the financial district of New York City think we've been out of the recession since 2009!

Meanwhile, the seniors who are the savers and investors—the people who actually worked to accumulate money for their retirement—have seen their safe money income choices pulled out from under their feet. Certificates of deposit in banking institutions now yield close to 0-percent returns. Both bank and brokerage firms offer money market accounts that pay nearly 0-percent interest.

The lack of a reasonable return on safe investments is coercing many conservative and frugal investors into making higher risk investments that are unsuitable for their age and risk tolerance. Everywhere we look there are ads promoting gold, exotic commodities, junk bonds, variable index annuities, highly leveraged stocks, and foreign currencies.

HOW WE CAN HELP YOU

If you are over 60 years old and you have lived your life as a conservative and frugal person, you need to know how to protect your lifestyle. You need help finding the right advice-givers. At our law firm, we have worked with hundreds of seniors and we have seen the financial choices that our clients have made.

They literally open up their books to us. We see our client-retirees' best, worst, but most often mediocre money decisions. We also get to evaluate the performance of their financial advisors, ranging from the big-time active-stock/bond money managers to the financial representative at the bank down the block. Regardless of their investment style, we have found that financial advisors' ideas also demonstrate the best, worst, but most often mediocre income-generation plans.

This book is meant to guide you as you cruise through retirement—from boomer, to senior, to elder. This is the guidance we provide our own clients every day. We know how to plan for the trip and predict the typical dangers. We're right there alongside our clients.

One thing we have learned for sure is that there are lots of potholes out there! As our client said at the beginning of this chapter, "They must have changed the rules." Quite frankly, "they" are always changing the rules—and we want to help you to avoid the hazards and slow down before the speed traps.

We'll show you how to synthesize safe financial ideas with visionary legal concepts. Our clients frequently tell us, "We don't want to be out of money before we are out of breath." It's our job to help you make that goal a reality.

We'll share with you what we've learned from the top 5 percent of financial advisors and estate protection attorneys. And we'll provide examples of the ideas our clients consider successful, our own "road maps" we follow so they can:

- Avoid becoming excessively impoverished by Alzheimer's disease, cancer, dementia, or other debilitating illnesses.

- Protect the lifestyle of the healthy spouse during the illness and after the death of their beloved partner.

- Create lifetime income and long-term care benefits with new hybrid insurance products coupled with innovative legal strategies.

- Provide lifestyle protection and then inheritance for adult children with disabilities and/or the education of grandchildren.

UNDERSTANDING WHAT YOU HAVE AND HOW MUCH YOU'LL NEED

Our good friend Matt Zagula, a nationally known author and respected financial advisor, asks this starter question: "What is your money for?" In other words, what basic goals do you have for what you have accumulated?

We often meet with clients and they provide a financial summary or statements showing their assets. These folks have raised their children, put them through school, paid for a home, completed a career, and now sit before us with a stack of papers that reveal to us what they have. But, as Matt points out, the important question is, "What's the money for?"

Some people have never really thought about it, perhaps because they were busy earning it, trying to invest it wisely, and in this economy trying not to lose it . . . spending some, saving some, worrying over it some. And now here they are with their net worth on paper.

When asked, "What's the money for?" we sometimes get a blank stare, a confused look, or at least a long pause. It may be that they haven't considered exactly what they have accumulated it for; or it may be that they've never tried to articulate it. No one has asked them to verbalize their hopes and dreams for the ride that's ahead of them.

Some have very specific plans, but most need to think about it.

We will prompt them by throwing out some ideas: "I suppose you would like to enjoy your retirement. Do you have any immediate plans?" This generally stimulates some conversation.

The man usually talks about being able to live comfortably during retirement, about not becoming a burden to his family, and about making sure that his wife has enough when he is gone. If he hasn't thought that far ahead, we discuss their income—what it is now and what it will be when only one of them remains. What income will be lost at the death of the husband? What income will be lost if the wife dies first? This can sometimes be a very eye-opening conversation.

You might be surprised to know that many couples don't understand that they will lose one Social Security check and possibly half (or even all) of the deceased spouse's pension income. Many people don't even know if their pension goes on to the surviving spouse, suffers a reduction, or stops completely. We point out that sometimes income drops by as much as two-thirds, while expenses barely diminish at all. Taxes are the same, utilities are the same, gas for the car is the same, and insurance on the house and car are the same. The only expense that may go down is the grocery bill. The cost of the supplemental healthcare insurance may be reduced; however, if the insurance was through the husband's pension and that is lost, now the wife must pay for a policy to supplement her Medicare.

Too often, the assumption is that if the couple has their home paid for and some money put away in savings and investments, they will be okay. But statistically, women most often outlive men of the same age. If Jim and Shirley are 65 and 63, it's likely that Shirley will need to be provided for at least five years after Jim dies. If Jim suffers from any long-term illnesses, it's likely they will have to dip into the funds they intended for Shirley. So when Jim dies, Shirley has less income and fewer assets, but nearly the same expenses.

Right after the stock market had a major drop in 2008, one client said, "My 401(k) is now my 201(k)." Financial experts counseled you to just leave your investments alone and they would eventually come back—that is, if you're young enough to wait that long. We were meeting with individuals and couples who didn't have that kind of time. Their income sources included Social Security, maybe a pension or maybe not, and interest and dividends that had all but dried up. The assets they had been counting on to take them through retirement were now drastically reduced.

Worse yet, Social Security, Medicare, and other programs baby boomers have been paying into for years, now face cuts or even elimination. More people are drawing from the government programs than paying in.

In the next few chapters we'll discuss these and other problems that seniors may face and how we cannot rely on the government to insure our retirement ride.

Chapter 2

LONGEVITY RISK

HOW TO PLAN FOR A VERY LONG LIFE

One of the biggest challenges of planning for retirement is predicting longevity. People are living much longer than they did even just a few decades ago. When Medicare was created in July of 1965, the majority of men died by the age of 65 and most women had passed away by age 72.

Today, everything is different. The good news is that we seniors have actually gained about 20 years—essentially a generation—of life. That's a real hallelujah! In fact, 50 percent of men who turned 65 in 2014 will live to age 84, and 50 percent of women will live to age 87. In addition, roughly 25 percent of women are expected to live beyond age 90. (Women typically outlive men of the same age by at least three years.)

Although longer life expectancy is a wonderful thing, it can present a real issue when trying to stretch retirement savings—possibly for 30 years or longer—for income needed to live on and keep up with the constantly rising cost of living.

We have seen clients make every possible mistake with their investments and their choice of financial advisor. Frankly, we have made our own mistakes—they say that's how we become wise. Wisdom most often is the result of surviving our own mistakes.

Yesterday's solutions and hot investment ideas are not a reliable guide for the road ahead. We are in a new economic time. The old ideas about investments, retirement, and estate planning are not working. If you're just looking back at yesterday's road map for success, you'll drive into the ditch. The rules of the road have changed. There's no use in looking back, so let's look at the road ahead.

Here are some key facts about basic investment instruments to keep in mind as you begin your journey. It pays to learn the pros and cons of each—it will really cost you if you don't.

ANNUITIES

Annuities are among the most misunderstood investments. Annuities are investment *contracts.* They are *not* equity investments like stock. They are *not* debt investments like bonds. They are contractual agreements between an insurance company and the purchaser. These contracts are written by insurance company lawyers, who often write in a way that's difficult for the layperson to understand.

Too many annuities are sold based on YTB, not ROI. "YTB" is our acronym for "yield to broker." "ROI" stands for "return on investment." ROI is return on investment to you.

Annuities are often misinterpreted by the buyer. The annuity salesperson often points out a bonus incentive, called a "bump," to buy the product. The salesperson tells the buyer that he/she will receive a 5-percent, 7-percent, or more bonus. The buyer mistakenly believes that the bonus is an actual cash value increase of added dollars. In reality, the bonus is an additional accounting ledger increase for determining the amount to be used for income payouts. It's a real bonus, but not as valuable as it's made out to be.

Insurance companies are required to maintain enormous capital reserves, and for that reason they have a historical record of surviving and thriving in both good times and bad. They are far better capitalized than any government, any bank, or almost any other type of company. (Apple or Google may have as high a percentage of reserves.) For investors with a low to moderately low risk tolerance who want to sleep soundly, life insurance company-underwritten annuities may be a safe choice.

When money is invested, the insurance company is forced to set aside legally defined reserves to underwrite the company's contractual obligation to pay you either for an insurance policy risk or for an amount of dollars defined in the annuity contract.

Reserves are specific to the individual insurance company's financial reserves and current surplus. State law governs the amount of reserves that are required to be held. It's not unusual for state regulators to require insurance companies to maintain a cumulative combination of both a reserve, plus a surplus (cushion) of $1.10 for every dollar received as a premium.

Life insurance companies have another advantage over banks and corporations as investments. Insurance companies do not pay taxes on their reserves, which are their invested assets. While they do pay taxes on their operating net income, the accumulations necessary to cover the policy obligations are treated as tax-exempt investments. This tax advantage provides the life insurance companies a significant benefit compared to banks, which must pay income tax on their investment-related profits.

Rick Says...

As a lawyer, I believe that no one should purchase an annuity without having it reviewed by an attorney who understands how to read and understand an annuity contract.

BONDS AND OTHER FIXED-INCOME DEBT

One of our favorite clients, Fern, called in a panic one day and breathlessly cried, "I've been defrauded! I bought some high-return bonds and this month's statement shows that I've lost a lot of money!" As we spoke with Fern it became obvious that she didn't understand what a bond is or how a bond's principal value can fluctuate wildly.

In the investment world, a bond is a security that represents a contract between a borrower (corporation, governmental body, banking institution) and a lender—*you*. A bond is usually a fixed-interest loan.

A bond loan arrangement uses terms that are unfamiliar to most. If you buy a bond, you are lending money to the borrower, who is the *issuer* of the bond. The bond loan terms detail what interest will be paid to the lender. The interest is called the *coupon*, and since the lender gets to hold the bond, they are called the *holder*.

The basic relationship between a borrower and lender is well-known to all. What makes a publicly traded bond so different is that the basic fundamental *principal* value of the bond fluctuates. Bond principal value fluctuations are caused by:

- The fixed-interest rate (coupon rate) of the bond compared to the ever-changing general market interest rates

- The perception of a change in the quality or reliability of the bond issuer/borrower

- The remaining term of interest payments

- The ability to easily buy and/or sell the bond (liquidity)

Fern had wanted a higher interest on her investment money than what she could receive from bank CDs and money markets. She went to a broker and emphasized that she wanted more *income*. He sold her some junk bonds.

It is important to understand that the term "junk bond" does not always mean that the bond is trash. Any high-yield bond that is not of a sufficient quality to be considered investment-grade is considered more risky and speculative. These bonds have a higher risk of the lender defaulting. They pay a higher rate of interest, but they are not the best choice for protecting widows and orphans, and Fern was a widow. She wanted higher income, but she was very risk-averse. When the value of her bond went down, she panicked and sold the bond at a loss—even though we had shown her that the actual income from the investment was still high, compared to the alternatives.

Today many baby boomers, seniors, and elders have moved trillions of dollars out of the stock market and fled to bonds of all types. Are these smart investments for a risk-averse retiree?

Since 2003, the U.S. federal government has been pushing interest rates down. Remember, the principal value of bonds is pushed *upward* when market interest rates move downward.

Sadly, our government has chosen to break the backs of frugal savers by killing a reasonable interest rate return. Temporarily, millions of bond investors who hold investment-grade bonds have enjoyed substantial gains in their bond funds. But what will happen now? The Federal

Reserve has reduced intrabank lending rates to an inflation-weighted negative yield. Real inflation is running between 3 and 10 percent per year,[1] while interest rate yields have been artificially depressed to 2 percent for a 10-year U.S. government bond.

How long can the government keep a lid on long-term interest rates? Whenever market interest rates begin to rise, the principal value of *all* existing bonds and bond funds will fall. No one knows how high interest rates will rise and bond values will fall, but the risk of great loss is a certainty.

Market interest rates have been artificially depressed for an extraordinarily long time. It does not take a Nostradamus to predict that rates must rise during the next few years. When that happens, millions of seniors will be echoing Fern's panic: "My statement shows that my principal has dropped!"

The interest income being paid on that bond will remain fixed, but the principal value fluctuates. Fixed-income bonds are not risk-free. They can be an important part of a retirement portfolio, but you must understand that *the principal value is not fixed; the income/interest* is fixed for the entire term of the bond.

---

1 Using the old governmental CPI formulae, many cite 10 percent or more as the *real* inflation rate.

Here at the end of 2014, everyone expects the Federal Reserve to raise interest rates in 2015. And while that may be correct, we've learned in the past that what everyone believes is seldom what actually happens. It may be that the Federal Reserve surprises everyone and does not raise rates for a long time. Right now, the junk bond market is responding to two apparent risk factors. Oil costs are temporarily plummeting and interest rates are expected to rise. When you combine those two concepts, suddenly trillions of dollars are moving out of speculative junk bond funds. Many seniors have purchased enormous amounts of junk bonds because they are desperate for a yield on their money. They can't get high yield in safe investments, so they have been forced to take greater risk than they want, and that's dangerous.

We may be at the beginning of a change in the historical cycle regarding high-yield bonds and a return to normal yields. For the last year or so, seniors have been buying high-yield bonds and now they're getting about a 6-percent return. Many of those seniors are just like our client Fern. She is a senior who wanted the interest rate but does not understand that when other interest rates go up, the principle value of a bond goes down. What will happen next, nobody can know for sure. It is very possible that we will see a substantial correction in the high-yield bond market and, if that happens, it could cause the stock market to decline substantially. That is just an opinion and not a fact. We are at a moment in the history of investing that has never existed before. For quite a long period of time, both stock market yields and bond yields have risen dramatically. Bonds are supposed to be the safe investment portion of a senior's asset portfolio. But at this particular moment, bonds have been acting in an abnormal and volatile manner. We have big concerns about the safety of seniors in the current market.

INFLATION'S IMPACT ON TRADITIONAL LOW-YIELD "SAFE" INVESTMENTS

All investments offer a balance between risk and potential return, and this balance tends to vary by the type of investment, the issuing entity, and the state of the economy. Bonds are no exception to this risk and return rule, although in some cases they are considered lower risk, especially compared to stocks. Some reasons for this include the fact that bonds offer a promise of returning the face value of the security to the holder at its maturity date.

Most bonds pay their investors a fixed rate of interest income. This income, just like the return of the bond's face value, is also backed by a promise from the bond's issuer. But, because of this "safety," bonds normally have historically lower average returns when compared with other investments. Therefore, investors need to be aware that even though bonds are considered to be "safe," this implied safety could be washed away by other unforeseen risks.

Of importance to retirees and others living on fixed incomes produced by bonds, there is interest rate risk. This means that when interest rates go up, the price of bonds falls. Conversely, when interest rates fall, the price of bonds goes up. Because of this, the longer the bond's maturity, the greater its interest rate risk.

Bonds also have something called duration risk. The modified duration of a bond is technically a measure of its price sensitivity to the movement of interest rates. This is primarily based on the average time to the maturity of its interest and principal cash flows.

Duration will allow an investor to more easily compare bonds with varying maturities and coupon rates by creating a simple rule. For example, for each percentage change in interest rates, the value of the bond will decline by its modified duration, stated as a percentage. For instance, an investment with a modified duration of five years will rise 5 percent in value for every 1-percent decline in interest rates, and it will fall 5 percent in value for every 1-percent increase in interest rates.

Another concern of retirees who are invested in bonds is inflation risk. This causes the dollar of tomorrow to be worth less than the dollar of today, essentially reducing a retiree's purchasing power. When living on a totally fixed income, with the constant increase in prices of goods and services, retirees cannot afford to take too much risk with their future purchasing power.

There are other types of risk that are associated with specific types of bonds. For example, bonds issued by a corporate, municipal, or government agency may possess "call" risk. This means they include a "call provision" that entitles their issuers to redeem them at a specified price on a date that occurs before the bond's actual maturity date.

Falling interest rates could accelerate the redemption of a callable bond, causing the investor's principal to be returned sooner than expected. In this case, the investor will have to reinvest the principal, likely at a lower interest rate. In addition, for a bond that is called either at or close to its par value, investors who paid a premium amount for the bond will also risk losing some of their principal.

Another type of risk that is associated with government agency, corporate, or muni bonds is liquidity risk. With liquidity risk, investors could have a difficult time finding a buyer when they want to sell. This may force the investor to sell their bond at a big discount to its market value. This risk is especially prevalent with lower rated bonds, bonds that are part of a small issue, and bonds that have recently had their credit rating downgraded.

Other issuers, such as those for corporate and municipal bonds and mortgage-backed or asset-backed securities, have specific types of risk as well. Credit risk, for instance, is the risk that the borrower will not be able to make interest payments when they are due, which could eventually lead to a default.

If a corporate debt issuer takes on a leveraged buyout, merger, or debt restructuring, it runs the gamut of event risk. This can happen if the underlying company takes on an additional debt load, which can cause the value of its bonds to fall or even interfere with its ability to make payments.

MORTGAGE-BACKED SECURITIES (BONDS)

Some risks associated specifically with mortgage-backed securities include prepayment risk, contraction risk, and extension risk. Prepayment risk entails the risk that declining interest rates or a strong housing market will cause the mortgage holders to refinance or otherwise repay their loans sooner than originally expected. This could then create an early return of principal to holders of these loans.

For mortgage-related securities, contraction risk is the risk that declining interest rates will accelerate the assumed prepayment speeds of mortgage loans, returning principal to investors sooner than originally expected and compelling them to reinvest at the prevailing lower rates.

Conversely, extension risk is the risk that rising interest rates will slow the assumed prepayment speeds of mortgage loans. This will essentially delay the return of principal to investors and could actually cause them to miss an opportunity to reinvest their funds at a higher yield.

TREASURY INFLATION PROTECTED SECURITIES (TIPS)

The U.S. government offers several types of government debt: treasury bills, treasury notes, treasury bonds, and Treasury Inflation Protected Securities (TIPS).

TIPS are unique in that the principal amount is adjusted according to the current formula used to calculate the Consumer Price Index (CPI). The principal can be adjusted upward or downward as inflation or deflation is determined. The interest rate remains the same. TIPS are offered for sale in maturities of five, ten, and thirty years.

During the recent past (2009–2010), the U.S. government calculated that the Consumer Price Index should remain *unchanged* due to the lack of inflation. As we previously discussed, many criticize the current CPI of being an inaccurate measure of the true impact of the cost of food, fuel, and housing. At the beginning of 2014, 30-year TIPS rates—reflecting the CPI—were about 1.5 percent. Now, a year later, they are about 0.7 percent. You be the judge: Has your cost of food, fuel, and housing increased at a rate slower than 1.5 percent over the last five years? Probably not. TIPS principal inflation adjustment may be a good idea, but will still significantly lag behind inflationary reality.

TIPS values are based on a government-manipulated formula that excludes the basic and inflation-sensitive commodities of food and fuel, meaning that you will not receive complete protection from inflation. As with so many things in life, the devil is in the fine print.

CERTIFICATES OF DEPOSIT (CDS)

Bank certificates of deposit (CDs) are another type of fixed-income investment over a predetermined term. Purchased from banks, credit unions, and most brokerage firms, CDs have been one of the safest and most popular retiree investments. They often provide a higher return than regular bank savings accounts. One important feature is that CDs are guaranteed by either the FDIC (for banks) or the NCUSIF (for credit unions). In the past, people were limited to choosing CDs from local banks, but today the internet greatly expands the possibilities. Websites such as www.bankaholic.com and www.bankrate.com can provide CD information and rate the banking institutions offering these rates.

In the not-too-distant past, CD investors were very reluctant to terminate a CD earlier than its maturity date because they didn't want to lose the interest that was earned only at the completion of the agreed certificate term. Since CDs are illiquid during the contractual term, one should always maintain sufficient money readily accessible for living expenses and modest emergencies.

During 2014, a typical six-month CD paid from 0.15 percent to 1.00 percent annual percentage yield (APY). A five-year CD yielded between 1.50 percent APY and a high of 2.25 percent APY. The best practice for CD investing has been to "ladder" the certificates of deposit.

A "CD ladder" is a series of CDs with staggered maturity dates. Retirees should consider "laddering" or "rolling" five-year maturity CDs. The goal is to have one CD maturing with full Interest every year. You are then free to either roll over the CD, choose some other investment, or spend the money. (As a note, this "laddering" or "rolling" concept can also be used to stagger bonds and fixed-income annuities.)

It's important to keep accurate records of your CD maturity dates to maximize your return on investment. Failure to take action usually results in an automatic roll-over of the CD that may not be at the highest interest rate available or be the best investment choice at the time.

The key advantages of a CD as an investment is *safety of principal.* The flip side is that current yields are taxable as ordinary income. The low interest rate yield is not sufficient to cover the cost of taxes and make up the loss of purchasing power of the principal caused by inflation.

Inflation is the biggest destroyer of the value of a CD. Over the last 50 years, the value of the U.S. dollar has declined by over 80 percent in purchasing power.

DIVIDEND-PAYING STOCKS CAN BE A WORTHWHILE EQUITY INVESTMENT

U.S. Treasury 10-year bonds currently have an annual yield of 2.05 percent. Higher returns can often be made in dividend-paying stocks. As of December 2014, in the Standard & Poor's 500 (the 500 largest capitalized companies whose shares are traded in the U.S.), 421 (or 84 percent) of the companies paid a dividend. Of those companies, 337 (67 percent of the S&P 500) increased their dividends within the previous year. In 2015, dividends per share are projected to grow approximately 8.3 percent. This is not so surprising when one analyzes big company earnings; their productivity and their profitability are rising dramatically as technological innovations allow companies to produce goods and services with fewer U.S. workers.

These companies are doing very well and have the confidence to raise dividends. In a sense, these dividend-paying stocks act as a hybrid or a "bond-like stock." The stock value is subject to the usual market valuation risks, but there is added value related to the income-producing power of the investment. On the downside, company management can increase and/or decrease the dividend payout at any time.

The studious investor can find many companies that have consistently paid dividends for years *and* have a pattern of increasing dividend yield per share. Some of the dividend-paying companies are the highest quality, multinational, business-dominating corporations. As far as stocks are concerned, these companies may be the safest equity investment choice. These companies are the likes of Walmart, Coca-Cola, Caterpillar, and Johnson & Johnson. They have substantial cash reserves, enormous positive cash flow, little debt, and they are present everywhere in the world.

With the downturn in the equity market and the success of these large corporations, it is possible that dividends will become an expectation of shareholders. In the boom-boom years between 1982 and 2000, dividends disappeared as equity values ballooned.

Retiree investors must seek out the strong and consistent dividend-paying corporations. If dividend yields increase, the stock price may advance for capital gains, too. Retirees must be first and foremost income investors; secondarily, they may also be stock growth investors. Unfortunately, a strong dividend-payer sinks when the tide rushes out, just like all the other boats.

If one looks for companies that have consistently paid out dividends, one can more likely predict what future *yields* will be paid than what the future stock *value* will be. Great dividend-paying companies pay yields *every quarter.* Some companies have increased their yield percentage year after year.

Every year, Standard & Poor's publishes a list of businesses that have actually raised their dividends for a minimum of 25 years (100 quarters). Companies on that list include Clorox, Automatic Data Processing, Coca-Cola, PepsiCo, McDonald's, Procter & Gamble, Abbott Labs, and Colgate.

If you are focused on income and can accept the nausea that comes from periodic stock market declines, then high-quality, dividend-paying stocks should be your focus for the share of your investment portfolio that is dedicated to equity.

WALL STREET'S STACKED DECK, OR "STRUCTURED INVESTMENTS"

> "Wall Street banks, Bank of America, Goldman Sachs and JP Morgan are the pimps of the world. First, they lend money to the government to purchase war material, then they lend money to industry so it can build warships and planes. Or do I have the order wrong?"
>
> —*Famed investment columnist Malcolm Berko*

Wall Street brokerage firms and banks have become empire-controlling forces that feed on investors of all sizes. Goldman Sachs and Merrill Lynch have been accused of selling inappropriate investments to pension funds for teachers and government employees. Wall Street watchdogs, Moody's, and Standard & Poor's rating services, are accused of giving the thumbs up to trillions of dollars of speculative derivatives that were exotic investments designed by Wall Street and then endorsed by the rating services—and are now worthless.

In order to further juice up their profits, the big brokerage houses now create "structured investment products," which are characterized as inexplicable and complex investments that will be highly promoted by unscrupulous salespeople due to the oversized commissions being paid. If your broker offers you a golden opportunity to purchase a structured investment, please run for the exit.

MUTUAL FUND COSTS ARE MISUNDERSTOOD AND NON-TRANSPARENT

Over the years, mutual funds have become a popular way for investors to get into the market without having to spend a lot of time managing their portfolio. That's because mutual funds are already managed portfolios, including diversified holdings in just about any type of industry or sector imaginable.

Over 80 million people—which equates to just about half of all U.S. households—invest in mutual funds, totaling trillions of dollars.

Even brand-new investors are able to get a well-diversified portfolio of equities, starting in some cases with as little as $25 or $100. In fact, mutual funds were originally touted as a great way for new investors to get into the market. Rather than spending hours on end reading over financial and stock data, all an investor needed to do was purchase a mutual fund.

Although in some cases investing in mutual funds is better than not investing at all, it is imperative to be careful and to read the fine print before doing so. This is because there are some drawbacks to investing in these funds that people need to be aware of.

Mutual funds in and of themselves are non-transparent investment vehicles. What this means is that these funds go out and buy things (shares of companies, in this case). In doing so, the fund has expenses of buying and selling. Other expenses of the fund, such as marketing and distribution, are bundled under the heading of 12B-1 fees.

Investors, as shareholders in the funds, are informed of what the fund has made or lost, and each investor in the fund absorbs their share of all the overhead and expense that is associated with it.

However, in many cases, when investors truly dig down into their mutual funds, they find information that's essentially beyond the prospectus—things such as trading costs, price, and execution expenses. These investors have also found that the fees are much higher than what they originally thought they were paying. For example, when investors were under the impression they were being charged annual fees in the 1 to 2 percent range, they may really have been being charged annual fees of closer to 3 or 4 percent—double the amount they thought. What this means to investors in mutual funds is that they must typically make between 3 and 4 percent as a hurdle just to break even.

Investors often feel that if they invest in "no-load" mutual funds, they will pay less in fees. This is not the case at all. In fact, a no-load mutual fund really just refers to the front-end load, not the annual load. What many investors are not aware of is that a no-load mutual fund may not have a front-end commission, but annual fees will more than likely make up for it. Many no-load mutual funds are actually running in excess of 2 to 3 percent extra per year above and beyond the operating expense that investors thought they were paying.

Another area where mutual fund abuses have been found is in the proprietary products offered by many financial institutions. Financial firms frequently offer only certain mutual fund families to their clients, stating that these funds are "preferred." This preferred status does not mean that these funds are the best. Rather, it means that the financial firm is likely making more commission by selling these particular funds to their clients.

There are other risks associated with mutual funds, such as manager risk. This refers specifically to the risk that a mutual fund may suffer as a result of poor, ineffective, or underperforming management. Essentially, this points to the fact that the mutual fund in and of itself may be a sound investment, however, the manager has made some poor decisions that have caused the fund price to fall.

Rick on Commodities and Highly Active Investing . . .

I am a nonstop student of investing and investments. I read *The Wall Street Journal almost every day.* I'm also a fan of Harry Markowitz, Ph.D. Economics, Dr. Steven Sjuggerud, and Dr. David Eifrig, Jr., and their investment concepts. I regularly check the interplay of various currencies compared to the U.S. dollar.

It has recently become apparent to me that commodity investments are *highly* correlated to stock market performance. For years, many investment advisors have advised that you should invest in real assets as a hedge (insurance) against a downturn in the stock market.

But during the last few years it has become obvious that, just as the S&P 500 moves up when investors are optimistic about the U.S. economy, so do the economy-related commodities of oil, natural gas, and silver. When investors become pessimistic about the economy, then both the stock market *and* the value of oil, natural gas, *and* silver fall.

In my experience with retirees who wished to pursue active investments, many of them had a misplaced faith that they could "beat the market." In most cases, the market beat them.

IS GOLD THE ANSWER?

During the recent economic downturn, there seemed to be a real push for people to purchase gold. It has been touted as being able to beat inflation and hold its value forever.

Yet gold may not be all it's cracked up to be as far as an investment. There a several reasons for this. First, unlike paper currency, whose value is impossible to manipulate, the same cannot be said about gold. In fact, by virtue of the fact that a group of connected buyers can accumulate the asset—essentially eliminating a large amount of its supply—a cornering of the market can take place, resulting in an upswing in price. After the upswing, however, these same buyers can soon sell the asset back out into the market again, replenishing supply and resulting in a huge drop in price. In this vein, it is important to remember that there is a limited supply of gold. And because of this, prices can be quite unstable. A similar situation occurred in the silver market in the 1980s. Although the likelihood of this happening again is slim, investors should still proceed with caution when considering purchasing gold as an investment.

In addition, for over two decades, the price of gold hardly moved at all. Investors who had invested in the commodity essentially wasted their time and their dollars, waiting for the value to rise. In the prior edition of this book, we stated that although the price of gold had recently risen due to the instability of the other financial markets, the gold rush was not likely to last. Those words have turned out to be prophetically true. Now that the stock market is reaching new highs, gold and other commodities have depreciated in value. At this particular moment, the price of gold is down. In addition, we now have a strong dollar, which makes it extremely expensive to carry gold. Although there are lots of gold bugs who will not be swayed by these facts, at this particular time and historically, gold has been a poor investment—especially for those in or near retirement.

Chapter 3

A WHOLE NEW ANGLE ON LONG-TERM CARE

OPTIONS FOR FUNDING YOUR FUTURE HEALTH NEEDS

Medicare does not provide long-term care. In chapter 4 we'll discuss more of the ins and outs of Medicare, but before we get into the strategies regarding long-term care, it is very important that you understand something about how Medicare is structured. When Medicare was born In July of 1965, seniors died primarily of causes that were classified as **acute care illnesses**, which means that you are expected either to get well quickly or to die quickly. Medicare was designed to be a source of funding for the five big killers of seniors: strokes, cancer, heart attacks, infectious diseases, and agricultural and industrial accidents. All of these medical killers are still around, but the bigger concern for seniors in 2014 is **chronic care illnesses**—illnesses or injuries from which you will never totally recover. The best you can hope for is that your chronic care illness is managed in a way that provides you with a longer life expectancy.

Today, we are greatly concerned about memory care, which was not a major issue in 1965. Memory care caused by dementia is the number-one driver of enormous healthcare expenditures by the federal government. In addition, memory care doesn't only mean a person is robbed of their memory—the sheer cost of care often robs them of their financial wealth, too. Medicare was not designed to provide care for clients at home, in assisted living, or in nursing homes.

Medicare will, however, continue to help pay for hospital visits, doctor visits, outpatient procedures, and drug costs during a senior's elder care journey. Medicare was never designed to cover the entire amount, so seniors need to at least purchase Medicare Supplement Insurance or a Medicare Advantage Insurance Plan. No senior should be without some type of supplemental coverage to pick up the huge deductibles of Medicare. The only seniors who are immune from great risk to Medicare deductibles are those who are "dual qualified," which means they are poor enough to qualify for both Medicare and Medicaid. Being dual qualified presents a new major problem, however: access to care. Due to the often poor paying habits of our state of Illinois, many physicians and quality healthcare providers refuse to provide care to those on Medicaid.

Well, if Medicare does not provide long-term care at home, assisted living, or nursing homes, how do we get reimbursement for care in those settings? If you do nothing, your wealth could be totally consumed by private pay for long-term care costs. Once you need help at home, assisted living, or a nursing home, you have a duty to pay for that cost of care out-of-pocket unless you have some sort of long-term care insurance coverage. In this country, somewhere between 4 and 7 percent of the population has sufficient long-term care insurance to provide quality care during their senior years. The only employees that we have met who have adequate long-term care insurance are typically employed by the United States Post Office or other federal agencies. If you are not employed by such an employer and you have no long-term care insurance, then this chapter offers some ideas on how to cover the enormous risk you face.

There are new types of products that may fit your situation and your finances. We have seen numerous clients who could not afford or did not choose to pay for traditional long-term care insurance who have peace of mind with these new products, which are linked to either a life insurance product or an income-producing annuity product. It seems like the insurance industry has finally gotten smart—they know that consumers do not want to purchase a product that is a "use it or lose it" situation. People want to know that, when they pay substantial amounts of money for coverage, if they don't end up needing long-term care insurance, there is still some value that goes either to them or to their surviving spouse or loved ones. The insurance industry has responded with the following concepts.

TRADITIONAL LONG-TERM CARE (LTC) INSURANCE: THE BENEFITS AND LIMITATIONS

When planning for the unexpected, long-term care (LTC) insurance should not be overlooked. This type of protection should be considered not only for its ability to pay for care services, but more so to protect and preserve assets.

Long-term care insurance protects assets, avoids dependency on others, and retains the insured person's freedom of choice. It is something that everyone needs to consider in the overall asset protection plan.

The benefits of owning an LTC insurance policy include:

- Asset and estate preservation
- Independence and integrity

- Flexibility and choice

- Easier access to care

Long-term care insurance can mean the difference between choosing the type of care that your client desires and deserves, or being forced to spend down assets in order to qualify for Medicaid.

Over the years there have been many changes and upgrades to LTC insurance policies. However, at its most basic level, the design of an LTC plan follows several parameters, and these factors also help to determine the premium cost of the policy. These factors include:

- **Applicant's age:** Long-term care insurance policies are priced based on the applicant's age. Sometimes this can be the actual age that the applicant is on the day that they complete the policy application for coverage, while other policies consider the applicant's age to be whatever their age is on their closest birthday.

- **Dollar amount of coverage:** Most LTC insurance policies are built around a daily dollar amount of coverage for care. This amount can be determined based on the applicant's income and expenses, as well as the approximate cost of care. It is important to determine how much income the applicant has coming in, as well as how much of that income he or she plans to put toward the actual daily expenses for the care received. As an example, if the average cost of care in a skilled nursing facility in an applicant's area is $200 per day, then the applicant may decide to insure for the entire amount of $200 per day, or he or she may decide to insure for only $100 per day of coverage and pay the other $100 per day out-of-pocket. Insuring for a lower daily dollar amount will keep the policy premium lower.

- **Inflation protection:** In addition to the daily dollar amount of coverage, the applicant also has the choice of leaving the dollar amount steady or increasing it each year. There are two choices for increasing the daily dollar amount of care: equal benefit increases or compound benefit increases. Both are typically increased in increments of 5 percent. What this means is that equal benefit increases will allow the original daily dollar amount chosen to increase by 5 percent of that amount each year. For example, if an applicant chooses a daily dollar amount of $100 per day, and they choose to have equal benefit increases, then their daily dollar amount of coverage will increase by $5 each year ($100 x 5 percent). The compound benefit increase means that the daily dollar amount will be compounded by 5 percent each year. In this case, each year the applicant's coverage will increase by 5 percent over the amount from the prior year. This option allows an applicant's daily amount to increase to larger amounts over the years. Usually the amount of coverage will continue to increase even after the insured person begins receiving benefits from the policy.

- **Elimination period:** Another pricing factor in LTC insurance policies has to do with the elimination period. This is the number of days that a policy owner must personally fund the care cost before the insurance benefits begin paying for care. This can be compared to the deductible in an auto insurance policy. There is not necessarily any set formula for determining the proper elimination period; it really depends upon how much of the care costs the policy owner wishes to fund before the insurance benefits begin to take effect. Some policies offer a 0-day elimination period, meaning that the insurance benefits will start on the first day of care that is received. Other choices can include 30-day, 60-day, 90-day, 100-day, or even 365-day elimination periods.

- **Duration of benefits:** Another factor in designing an LTC plan is the duration of benefits. Most LTC policies offer a lifetime benefit option. This means that benefits will continue through the duration of the policy owner's life. An applicant can also choose a certain number of years for their care coverage. Benefit duration options include one year, two years, three years, five years, six years, or ten years. Since one of the primary purposes of LTC insurance is to protect against catastrophic illness, longer benefit periods should be considered. However, the amount of other income that the policy holder has to use toward paying for care will also factor into this determination.

Even though an individual may have an LTC insurance policy, there are certain requirements that must be met in order to trigger the benefits from a plan. Unlike older policies, however, in most cases no prior hospitalization is required, as is with Medicare skilled nursing home coverage.

Most LTC insurance policies will require that the policy holder either:

- Needs continual assistance with a certain number of activities of daily living (ADLs), or

- Needs continual supervision due to a cognitive impairment.

Activities of daily living (ADLs) include eating, dressing, bathing, transferring, toileting, and continence. "Cognitive impairment" is defined as the deterioration or loss of intellectual capacity that is evidenced by memory loss, disorientation and/or the ability to reason. It is often caused by Alzheimer's disease or similar forms of senility or irreversible dementia. When a person is unsafe in a normal environment, he/she is in need of full time assistance in a protected environment.

ANNUITY-BASED LONG-TERM CARE

Many of our clients are finding that annuity-based long-term care is the right answer for them. The concept of using annuities to obtain long-term care was authorized during the second President Bush administration. On August 17, 2006, the Pension Protection Act was created. Under that act, it became possible for a person to own an annuity contract, which could provide long-term care if an individual purchased an appropriate "rider," or added provision, to that annuity. What was especially exciting about that act was that, for the first time, seniors were allowed to use their IRA or other qualified funds to purchase annuities with LTC riders. Up to that time, IRAs could not be used to purchase LTC insurance. As with all things political, the government can redefine how to achieve certain goals.

The important thing about the Pension Protection Act is that now you may be able to use the cash value of an annuity to pay premiums on LTC insurance. The act allows annuity contracts without LTC riders to be tax-free exchanged for other annuity contracts that have an LTC rider. Such an exchange is tax-fee under Section 1035 of the Internal Revenue Code. This idea may be important to those who already own an annuity with a high value and who are now not healthy. In this situation, the cash value of the annuity can be used to purchase LTC insurance.

We have had the good fortune of working with Don Quante, an expert in LTC insurance. Mr. Quante has written a book, *Don't Go Broke in a Nursing Home!*, which was edited for Illinois by Rick Law. You may contact Mr. Quante through his website, www.dontgobroke.com.

In his book, he provides an example of how an annuity-based long-term care plan could help someone. For this example, we will call our client Bob, age 70 and recently widowed. His children live out of town, and they were very concerned about what would happen if Dad needed some additional care in the future. Since Bob had some health concerns and was recently diagnosed with diabetes, along with a history of heart disease, he was not a good candidate for traditional LTC insurance. However, by taking advantage of an annuity-based long-term care strategy under the Pension Protection Act, Bob could likely be insured by a new style of product. Bob had a $140,000 fixed annuity with a cost basis of only $40,000. The cost basis, in this case, was the amount he had actually paid for the annuity in the beginning. He was able to use a Section 1035 tax-free exchange, which rolled over his existing fixed annuity to a new annuity that complied with the rules laid out in the Pension Protection Act. Bob's $140,000 fixed annuity continued to earn interest. However, if he needed long-term care to pay for homecare, assisted living, or skilled care, he now had a long-term rider, which would provide money equal to $280,000.

It's important to understand that, depending on the real facts and circumstances, in some cases someone in Bob's situation might not be provided with this much care based on his rollover. On the other hand, depending on other facts and circumstances, other individuals may receive even more money toward their cost of care. In every situation, the insurance company is going to look at the patient's health and history, as well as the current economic market, to do the math and determine what they believe is in the best interest of the insurance company.

Rick on When an Annuity is Right for You . . .

In our long experience in working with seniors, we've seen that 90 percent of the annuities that are sold are dangerous to their financial health. On the other hand, it's important that you understand what's wrong with the 90 percent of annuities so that you can recognize the top 10 percent of those annuities, which may be a winner for you.

Here's a brief overview of the four basic types of annuities:

- **Fixed annuities** are investments issued by insurance companies that are primarily geared toward retirement savings, promising the investor a fixed series of payments for a predetermined length of time. There are many types of fixed annuities, which vary in when premiums are paid and how benefits are paid out.

- **Variable annuities** provide the opportunity for market appreciation through a variety of investment options, with tax-deferred accumulation as well as future income. Factors to consider when shopping for variable annuities are fees, fund choices, surrender charges, performance over time, and financial strength of the issuing company.

- **Indexed annuities** have returns based upon the performance of an equity market index, such as the Dow Jones, the S&P 500, or the NASDAQ. The investor's principal investment is protected from losses in the equity market, while the gains add to the annuity's return. These products are not considered liquid investments, and in most cases, they have formidable surrender charges. Indexed annuities are private contracts and are not traded in the open market.

- **Hybrid annuities** have both fixed and variable components. Federal law has made the **Single Premium Immediate Annuity (SPIA)**, a hybrid annuity that is often used to provide help to a healthy spouse when their ill spouse needs nursing home Medicaid. The client writes a check for the total amount of the investment, and the annuity company takes the client's money and pays it back month-to-month in equal payments over a determined period of time. This product takes the money that would have been counted as an asset—preventing the client from qualifying for public benefits—and turns that asset into an income stream over a specific period of time. The monthly income is determined by the term and the amount placed into the annuity, and this is all determined by the particular need of the client.

As you can guess, we're barely scratching the surface of these annuities and what they can do for you if used well. Remember that annuities are contractual investments offered by life insurance underwriters. The contracts offer certain benefits and *they always have strings attached.* Beware of deceptive salespeople and fraudulent practices—the area of annuities has encountered its share of both of these. Every investment choice has a pro and a con. Our job is to understand the pros and the cons so that we can help each client make the best choice.

LIFE INSURANCE WITH A LONG-TERM CARE RIDER

Another important concept to understand is life insurance with a long-term care rider. Traditionally, LTC insurance policies were of the use-it-or-lose-it variety. The typical LTC insurance product was sold to cover one kind of risk: long-term care costs. If you did not use the insurance, you got nothing at the end of your life. Now, insurance companies are offering combination products, which use life insurance as the chassis upon which they add the accessories of LTC insurance. This concept has not been available until recently. Like the annuity with the LTC rider, the life insurance with an LTC rider is often referred to as a linked insurance product. The insurance industry has designed hybrid products that link an LTC benefit with either a life insurance policy or an income-oriented annuity.

When it comes to using a life insurance product as a vehicle for long-term care, the insurance company will allow the insured to basically use some of the death benefit of the life insurance policy if the insured is unable to perform two of the six ADLs (eating, dressing, bathing, transferring, toileting, and continence). The trump card of ADLs is when a person has dementia, and they are unsafe in a normal environment.

The most attractive feature of using life insurance to get long-term care is the ability of the insured to use the money to pay for home healthcare, assisted living, or nursing home care. The policy may even allow for you to pick who your caregiver is, including family members.

Let's look at an example. Sue is a 55-year-old woman; she is a single mom, and she has children who are now adults. She has an existing life insurance policy, but has no long-term care coverage. Sue is very concerned about what is going to happen to her when she needs long-term care; she has no one at home to provide care for her, so she might need to go to a nursing home. She would like to be able to buy some LTC insurance, but she has checked into the cost and she does not feel that she can afford the premiums. A possible solution could look like this: Sue could replace the cost of her existing insurance product—she could use the premiums she pays for that product to purchase another life insurance policy. If she were able to purchase a replacement insurance policy with an LTC rider, she would be able to choose where she wants to be able to receive her care. If she does not use the LTC benefit, she would be able to provide a tax-free benefit to her children from the life insurance proceeds when she passes away. Calculations on this concept would be based on facts and circumstances. We have seen many situations where clients have replaced existing insurance policies with new insurance policies that provide some LTC benefits and in many cases have wound up paying no more annual premiums for the new products than they were paying for the old products.

Zach's Tax Tips for Choosing Your Own Caregiver . . .

You can hire a child or a loved one to be your caregiver while you're alive, but in order to avoid consequences, it must be done in the right way. Here are a few tips:

- Make sure the caregiver claims your payments as income—otherwise it's considered a gift for Medicaid purposes.
- The parent (or person getting care) should set up withholding like a business, including social security, workers comp, and the like. This is technically subject to the household employee income tax rules as detailed in IRS Publication 926, which is updated annually on the IRS website.

- Familiarize yourself with the relevant laws and regulations. There is an Illinois law which states that if care is provided by a relative for a relative, that the care is presumed to have been provided due to love and affection. Failure to understand this law can lead a family member to be unfairly accused of elder abuse and/or theft.

ASSET-BASED LONG-TERM CARE

Many times when we meet with clients, we find that they have accumulated assets that are not necessary to support their lifestyle. About 20 percent of our clients expect their assets in their cash value life insurance and their IRAs to outlive them and their surviving spouse. Some of these monies could be allocated toward the purchase of a product that would give them an asset *and* a long-term care benefit.

When we were young, we often bought life insurance for the unlikely, but catastrophic possibility that we would die leaving our spouse and children without a provider. For our seniors who do not have LTC insurance, the greatest risk to destroying their assets in their retirement years is the un-reimbursed cost of healthcare. And at least for today, the number one risk to those assets is long-term care diseases, such as Alzheimer's and Parkinson's. Many of our clients have chosen not to buy LTC insurance because they decided that paying annual premiums was unnecessary and too expensive. What they chose instead was to state that they had sufficient assets to self-insure. What they mean by that is they will pay out-of-pocket for long-term care.

These individuals could benefit from investing some of their assets in such a way that would actually enhance the overall likelihood of more money being available for the next generation. In addition, this money would be available to help pay for in-home, assisted living facility, or nursing home care. If the money is not needed for this purpose, it would then pass to the next generation. There would be no "use it or lose it" issues, as there are with conventional LTC insurance.

To use this strategy, money is transferred from its current location (bank account, fixed annuity, etc.) into a very carefully designed life insurance policy with riders that prepay the death benefit, and additionally can be used to reimburse the insured for the enormous cost of long-term care. Depending on age, sex, and health status, the money paid into one of the policies may be worth twice as much if the insured dies without ever needing to use it. Also, if needed for facility care, the insured can receive up to two to five times the amount of money deposited into the contract. Any money not used for that purpose would then pass to the heirs at death.

One of the most amazing parts about this concept is that while clients are invested in this type of insurance policy, their money is available to them for any other reason at any time. Most of these products are written with a money-back guarantee that ensures that the policyholders will always have access to their funds in the event they have a change of mind due to a change of circumstances. Rather than a typical insurance product, the transaction is more like repositioning your money from one account to another. Within the insurance product, you can have a cash value account that provides a type of savings feature. This is not a bank-insured product; rather, it is backed by the assets and reserve of the insurance company. It is prudent to make sure that you are buying a product from a very reputable, highly rated insurance company.

The actual cost of long-term care is significant (potentially $85,000 to $120,000 per year or more here in Illinois), especially when the need for care extends over long periods of time: the average care need for a man exceeds two years, and for a woman it exceeds five years. Thus, these policies are usually purchased with a rider that extends the LTC benefits after the death benefit has been exhausted. These riders can effectively double or triple the benefit in the event that a person lives a long, long time.

This approach may be ideal for some individuals who reject the idea of purchasing conventional, annual-premium LTC insurance policies. Again, what is actually available to you is not determinable until you have made an application with an insurance company. Through our firm, we work with a number of reputable insurance agencies that represent some of the major insurance companies in the country.

Of all the contingencies and risks facing retirement, long-term care is probably the most difficult and perhaps the most costly. It is costly financially, and it is extremely costly emotionally. It can be devastating to the person with the unwelcome diagnosis and their spouse and children. These asset-based LTC strategies allow you to manage your money in such a way that you can provide significantly for long-term care possibilities without having to pay large annual insurance premiums. When you have sufficient margin, this may be the most painless way to reallocate some of your portfolio so that you can retain control of the value and achieve LTC coverage through a safe and risk-reducing option.

LONG-TERM CARE PRODUCTS PURCHASED USING IRA MONIES

The last strategy that we're going to discuss is the long-term care products purchased using IRA monies. While most people use their IRA to supplement retirement, many times waiting until age 70½ (at which point the mandatory required minimum distribution rules apply), some people have chosen to take a portion of their IRA and fund an IRA-based LTC policy.

As an example we will use Tim, age 60, recently widowed and retired. While he feels very secure about his retirement income, his main concern is long-term care. By taking advantage of a tax-free, IRA Trustee/Custodian to IRA Trustee/Custodian transfer of assets, Tim repositions $157,000 of his $500,000 IRA account into an IRA-based LTC policy. After Tim makes this $157,000 transfer, the new product immediately guarantees a $167,000 death benefit to Tim (including a $10,000 bonus benefit from the insurance company), or a $6,976 monthly income when and if Tim is diagnosed as needing professional help due to aging long-term care needs.

Here's an example of a married couple who uses an IRA-based LTC plan. Beth is 60 and Bob is 65, and they are concerned about long-term care. Up to this point, they may have been scared away from purchasing traditional LTC insurance due to the cost of annual premiums. In their situation, they find that they do not need additional income from Bob's IRA. They are wondering how they can use their IRA to help their children. In addition, they would like to avoid having their children pay the high cost of taxes on their IRA account when both Bob and Beth have passed away. They understand that *someone* is going to pay taxes on the IRA; they just wish that the value could be passed on to their children in a tax-free manner. This is a great way for them to accomplish that goal and to get long-term care at the same time: they could take advantage of a tax-free, trustee-to-trustee transfer of some of their IRA assets. If Bob decides to transfer $240,000 from his $500,000 IRA into an IRA-based LTC policy, he could achieve some big benefits. Upon the death of both Bob and Beth, their children will receive a tax-free death benefit in the amount of $436,000. That number is given purely for example purposes. Actual numbers vary depending upon the facts and circumstances. In this example, Bob has made a transfer of $240,000 of his IRA into another IRA account. His actual net worth has not declined. In addition, by making this transfer, Bob and Beth have been promised an $8,716 monthly long-term care benefit applicable to both of them to be used to pay for home healthcare, assisted living, adult daycare, or even skilled nursing home care. In addition to those benefits, should they ever need to withdraw their $240,000, the policy offers a full refund of premium.

In working with our clients, we have seen a wide variation on this particular example. The bottom line is that it is well worth the person's while to review this portion of their retirement planning to make sure that this particular risk has been addressed. This will not work for everyone.

You can only buy long-term care insurance with two things: your health and your wealth. For situations where the concepts discussed in this chapter fit, it puts a smile on the face of our clients and provides them with great piece of mind knowing they have achieved some sort of long-term care that will benefit not only them, but also their survivor spouse and/or beneficiary children.

Chapter 4

MEDICARE: THE DOLLARS AND CENTS

WHAT YOU NEED TO KNOW ABOUT MEDICARE SO YOU WON'T LOSE YOUR HOME

CO-AUTHORED WITH THE ESTEEMED MICHAEL LEWIS (SEE HIS BRIEF BIOGRAPHY IN APPENDIX 1)

Medicare provides acute care, hospital coverage, outpatient coverage, prescription drug coverage, hospice, durable medical equipment, and more. Nonetheless, Medicare does not pay for 100 percent of *any* of these areas of coverage. Even if you qualify for what's referred to as "Original," "Traditional," or "Regular" Medicare, if you don't have some type of supplemental coverage, you risk losing everything to unreimbursed medical expenses. The goal of this chapter is to make sure you understand what Medicare covers and what it does not cover. We wish this chapter could be less technical; nonetheless, we have striven to provide you with clarity.

OVERVIEW OF MEDICARE SUPPLEMENT PLANS (MEDIGAP) AND ADVANTAGE PLANS

Let's start with what are referred to the ABCs of Medicare Supplement Insurance plans. Many seniors are covered by Original Medicare (which partially covers Parts A and B below), and they then purchase a Medicare Supplement Insurance, also called "Medigap," to increase their coverage. Medicare is made up of three distinct parts:

1. Medicare Part A benefits

    - services furnished as an inpatient hospital admission
    - post-hospital rehabilitative services in a skilled nursing facility
    - home health agency services
    - hospice care

2. Medicare Part B benefits

- physicians and other provider services
- outpatient hospital services
- diagnostic services, such as laboratory, x-rays, and EKGs
- durable medical equipment

3. Medicare Part D benefits

- outpatient prescription drug services obtained by you from your pharmacist

You automatically receive **Medicare Part A** benefits at no additional cost when you are eligible for Social Security benefits. Oftentimes boomers do not qualify for Social Security benefits until after age 65, in which case they may qualify for Medicare Part A benefits prior to the time they qualify for full-retirement-age Social Security benefits. If you do delay your Social Security benefits beyond the age of 65, it is critical that you still apply for Medicare Part A benefits at the age of 65.

Medicare Part B benefits are obtained when you apply for them. You pay a monthly premium, which is deducted from your Social Security check. In the event that you do not receive Social Security, you will write your own check for Part B benefits.

Your **Medicare Part D** benefits—your prescription drug plans—are available when you turn 65. You obtain the benefits from private insurance companies that have contracted with a Medicare program to provide the insurance. You pay an additional premium for Medicare Part D benefits, and the payment is made to the appropriate insurance company chosen by the individual.

Rick on Medicare Supplement Plan F . . .

Medicare Supplements are standardized and labeled from A to N. Even though we typically see A as the best or superlative and F as a failure, when it comes to Medicare Supplements, F is the best plan. Plan F essentially covers whatever your Original Medicare did not cover. Please note that this is a supplement, so Plan F covers everything *after* Original Medicare has approved the initial charges; if Original Medicare does not approve your initial charges, then the supplement pays nothing. Under Medicare Plan F, you are not restricted to networks. Your Original Medicare and Medicare Supplements are accepted everywhere that Medicare is accepted. That allows you to choose to go to Mayo or Cleveland Clinic. That is a huge benefit. Original Medicare and Medicare Supplements insurance are accepted everywhere. If you have Plan F, there are no deductibles and no co-pays. According to my sources in the Chicago metropolitan area, 60 to 65 percent of seniors have Blue Cross Blue Shield Plan F as their Medicare Supplement.

An ever-growing percentage of boomers—some reports indicate about 50 percent—purchase a **Medicare Advantage Plan (Medicare Part C)**, which is an alternative to Original Medicare. Medicare Advantage Plans are privately-owned, HMO-like Medicare programs that normally include all the benefits of Medicare Part A, Part B, and most of the time, Part D. Medicare C is offered by certified insurance companies that have contracts with the Medicare program. You may choose to obtain a Medicare Advantage Plan in place of Original Medicare. We will discuss Medicare C, it's advantages and disadvantages, toward the end of this chapter.

Now that you have a general idea of the ABCs of Medicare, let's have a look at some of the details you'll need to know as you are deciding how to best use Medicare to your advantage.

MEDICARE PART A (HOSPITAL INSURANCE)

Medicare Part A helps pay for inpatient hospital stays, care in a skilled nursing center, hospice care, and some home health care. Under Medicare Part A, your initial inpatient **hospital admission** would have you pay the initial inpatient deductible, which for 2015 is a maximum of $1,260. After that, all other services from admission day 1 through day 60 are paid in full. If you have an admission that goes from day 61 through day 90, you would have to pay a $315 co-pay each day. (If you have a Medicare Supplement or Medicare Advantage Plan, it may help cover that deductible.) After day 91, you are responsible to cover all costs. Through Medicare Part A you do have 60 "lifetime reserve days" that you can use to carry you through day 150. These lifetime reserve days require a daily co-pay of $630 a day; however, once you have used those 60 days, you would never receive any additional of those days for any future admissions under Medicare Part A.

One of the most important things to understand and recognize about the Medicare Part A program is the definition of an inpatient admission versus hospital observation status. The definition may adversely affect your maximum benefits under Medicare Part A, and also any post-hospital admissions for rehabilitative services in a skilled nursing care facility. Being designated as under "hospital observation" rather than as an inpatient has become one of the biggest problems for Medicare recipients.

Rick on the Cost of Outpatient Status . . .

In our practice, we have noticed that since October of 2012, there is a rising pressure from Medicare upon hospitals to admit Medicare recipients as observation status only. In our opinion, the reason for this pressure is to lessen the cost on the federal government for Medicare recipients. If you are classified as being in the hospital under observation, your Medicare *Supplement*—rather than Original Medicare—must pay much more than if you're in the hospital as an admitted patient. In addition, if you are not *admitted* to the hospital, when you are released you will need to pay privately out-of-pocket for any post-hospital rehabilitative services in a skilled nursing care facility. We have had clients in this circumstance who have paid between $41,000 and $110,000 out-of-pocket in additional expenses.

We know of clients who have undergone hip-repair surgery and spent more than six days in the hospital. Nonetheless, they were treated as having been in the hospital under observation, not as an inpatient. In our experience it has been impossible to retroactively change the status from observation to admitted patient. We believe that the federal government is playing word games to the detriment of Medicare recipients across the country.

Unfortunately, hospitals are not required to inform the patient or the family that the individual has been designated as an outpatient under observation status rather than an admitted inpatient. It is critical that, as soon as the patient is placed in a room, the patient or the patient's family member immediately get in touch with the hospital admissions office and the patient's family doctor to ensure that the hospital appropriately designates the stay as *inpatient* hospital admission. If the status is not changed at this time, once a diagnosis is rendered the family should again talk to the doctor and the admissions department to get the admission changed from outpatient observation to admitted inpatient. (Note that, under Medicare, an inpatient hospital stay must include a minimum of three days or two midnights in the hospital as an admitted patient.) A patient who does not take this action could, at the time he is leaving the hospital, find out that his stay at the hospital is classified as outpatient observation. When this occurs, it is very difficult to get the hospital to change its designation and requires significant involvement of the patient and family member with the hospital and the Medicare program.

If a patient's stay at the hospital is classified as an observation status, then the patient would be responsible for 20 percent of the hospital charges for the time stayed at the hospital. Most often that is covered by your Medicare Advantage or Medicare Advantage Plan. However, more issues arise if the patient must be transferred to a post-hospital rehabilitative facility, for example, a skilled nursing home facility. When a patient has been admitted to a **skilled nursing facility** for post-rehab services, and it *is* covered by Medicare Part A, the patient will pay nothing for the first 20 days of skilled nursing care. From the 21st day to the 100th day the patient will be responsible to pay a deductible of $157.50 per day. If for some reason the patient continues to stay in the nursing rehab facility, beginning on the 101st day, the Medicare

Part A program provides no additional coverage. This is why it is critically important to qualify for Medicare coverage starting with your hospital stay: if you are in the hospital only under observation status, later when you enter a skilled nursing facility, you're in the same category as the person who has received Medicare Part A program coverage for 100 full days in the same facility. Unfortunately, if you do not qualify for Medicare Part A post-hospital rehabilitative skilled facility care, you are on your own from day 1.

Once a patient has been discharged from a skilled nursing facility, and the patient has not had an inpatient hospital stay or a subsequent skilled nursing facility stay for a total of 60 consecutive days, then all benefits get renewed under the skilled nursing facility program. Many people at the time of the decision to be admitted to a skilled nursing facility do not really know the best facility to be transferred to for their rehabilitative care. As a patient, the best way to know that you're getting the best quality care from a particular skilled nursing facility is to go to the Medicare webpage, www.medicare.gov, which provides quality indicators for the skilled nursing facilities in your geographic area. Also, a patient can obtain a publication which provides good information about skilled nursing care. This publication can be obtained through the Medicare website or simply by typing the title of the publication, "Medicare Coverage of Skilled

Nursing Facility Care," into Google.com or a similar search engine.

Medicare Part A also helps cover certain **services furnished by a home health agency**. These are not long-term home healthcare services. To obtain such care, your physician must have a face-to-face interview with you, and the physician must order the services and prepare a written order known as a "plan of care." Also, you must be homebound. This means you're normally unable to leave home, and doing so requires a considerable and taxing effort and is not medically advisable. Once again, this is a rehabilitative program for you to heal from an acute care illness—not for long-term care.

The last benefit under Medicare Part A is **hospice care**. To qualify for hospice care, a hospice doctor and your personal doctor must certify that you are terminally ill and expected to live six months or less. Hospice care coverage under Medicare includes all items and services needed for pain relief and symptom management; medical, nursing, and social services; drugs; and certain durable medical equipment, such as a hospital bed. It does not include the cost of the facility care. You can receive hospice care in your home or other facility where you live, such as an assisted living center or a nursing home. You will pay a co-payment of up to $5 per prescription for outpatient drugs used for pain and symptom management while on hospice care, as well as 5 percent of the Medicare-approved amount for any inpatient respite care. Under the hospice care program the patient can get up to five days of inpatient respite care in a Medicare-approved facility to allow the patient's usual caregiver to get rest.

MEDICARE PART B (MEDICAL INSURANCE)

Medicare Part B covers outpatient hospital, physician, diagnostic, and laboratory services. You can get Medicare Part B benefits when you initially apply for Social Security benefits or initially apply for Medicare. There are specific timeframes to obtain Medicare Part B. Typically, you would have a Medicare Part B monthly premium subtracted from your Social Security check, or you may pay it directly for the premium if you do not qualify for Social Security benefits. It is important to note that you will pay $104.90 per month if your current yearly income is $85,000 or less for an individual filing under federal taxes (or you're married filing separate tax returns), or you have an income of $170,000 or less for a joint filing. Your yearly income is classified as the modified adjusted income (MAGI) that you reported to the IRS two years prior to the application.

If your MAGI is greater than the amounts previously stated, there will be an additional amount deducted from your Social Security check on top of the standard premium of $104.90. In essence, if you have what the federal government considers to be a high income, you will experience a higher cost for Medicare Part B and, looking ahead, a much higher cost for the prescription drug program. This is part of the way the federal government imposes a hidden tax on people with higher incomes. It's important to know what the income thresholds are as you are doing retirement income planning because the receipt of substantial monies from various types of financial planning can substantially increase your MAGI, causing you to have much higher costs for both Medicare Part B and the prescription drug plan. In addition to these higher costs, there are financial penalties if you decide to delay getting Medicare Part B. If you delay and then subsequently enroll under Medicare Part B, you will pay a higher Medicare Part B monthly premium for life.

There are common exceptions to this delayed enrollment rule. The exceptions are classified as life-changing events. If a beneficiary initially enrolls under Social Security and the individual had medical coverage through their employer or through their spouse's employer, then the individual would not necessarily enroll under Medicare Part B. However, if later the beneficiary loses the other medical insurance, then this would be classified as a life-changing event, and the beneficiary would apply for Medicare part B under the exception rule. The beneficiary normally has 63 days from the date of terminating the previous insurance to apply for Medicare Part B.

The 2015 out-of-pocket costs under Medicare Part B program are as follows:

1. You pay the first $147 of covered Medicare Part B services per calendar year.

2. After paying the initial $147, you normally pay 20 percent of the Medicare-approved amount for subsequent covered Part B services.

3. Medicare Part B pays 100 percent of the outpatient clinical laboratory services.

There is substantial confusion among Medicare recipients about the difference between a "medical charge" compared to the "Medicare-approved amount" mentioned in number two. Normally, a Medicare-approved amount is different from the provider's normal charge. For example, say you went to see your physician for what is known as an established level-4 office visit. The physician's normal charge is $194, but the Medicare-approved amount is $114.53 under the current Medicare B schedule. Therefore, the maximum amount the physician would receive from Medicare, you, or your Medicare Supplement Insurance program is $114.53.

The difference between the $114.53 and the physician's normal charge of $194 is $79.47, which would be subtracted from your bill by your physician. In summary, the maximum that you and Medicare would pay to your physician is $114.53, and the physician could not ask you to pay any additional amount for the covered Medicare Part B services.

Please note that this example applies only when the physician submits a claim to Medicare Part B and has a participating agreement with Medicare Part B. If you see a Medicare physician who has determined not to participate in Medicare, then the maximum amount that the physician can charge you would be 115 percent of the Medicare-approved amount. So, for the example stated above, if the Medicare-approved amount is $114.53, then the amount the physician can charge you is $131.71. However, Medicare would pay directly to you the Medicare-approved amount, subject to the Medicare Part B deductible and the Medicare co-insurance amount.

Remember that Medicare does not pay for everything and does not pay for all services. When Medicare does not pay for medical service, such as cosmetic surgery or routine preventive visits that have not been classified as a Medicare well visit, then you will have to pay the actual, full charge that the physician requires for the service, not the Medicare-approved amount. The following are medically necessary services that are covered by Medicare and subject to the Medicare Part B deductible, paid at 80 percent of the Medicare-approved amount:

- Physician office visits
- Physician outpatient hospital visits
- Physician inpatient visits
- Physician surgical procedures
- Ambulance services
- Physician anesthesia services
- Durable medical equipment
- Second opinion services before surgery
- Ambulatory surgical center charges
- Artificial limbs, eyes, braces, prostheses
- Cardiac rehab program
- Chemotherapy services and related chemotherapy drugs
- Medically necessary chiropractic services

- Cosmetic surgery because of accidental injury or to improve the function of a malformed body part

Medicare Part B covers diabetes services and supplies; diagnostic tests such as EKGs, X-rays, MRI, CT Scan, and Ultrasound services; outpatient dialysis services; and healthcare workers such as physician assistants, nurse practitioners, clinical nurse specialists, clinical social workers, and clinical psychologists. Medicare Part B also pays for the emergency room hospital charges and, if the patient has been designated as a hospital observation status, Medicare Part B would provide coverage. However, under hospital observation status, the patient is responsible for the initial inpatient deductible if not previously paid for the calendar year, and the patient is responsible for 20 percent of the hospital observation charges.

It's important to note that Medicare Part B does not provide any payment for oral prescription drugs furnished by the hospital during a hospital observation stay. This means that, if you're in the hospital and you are given oral prescription drugs such as aspirin, you will be billed at the hospital rate. There have been articles written about how hospitals routinely jack up the cost of oral prescription drugs by hundreds if not thousands of percentage points. In addition, they will most often refuse to allow you to use the oral prescription drugs that you have in your own possession.

Medicare Part B also pays for outpatient physical therapy, speech therapy, or occupational therapy. However, for these services there is a maximum Medicare payment plan per year. Also, Medicare Part B deductible on the 20-percent patient co-pay applies to these outpatient therapies. If you happen to go into Chicago and receive physician services in an outpatient hospital setting, such as one of our many university medical centers, you would be responsible for two bills: First you would pay for the physician's 20-percent co-pay and then the related 20-percent co-pay for outpatient hospital visits.

The Part B program also covers 100 percent of the Medicare-approved amount of some clinical laboratory tests, such as a urinalysis or a blood test.

What if Medicare will not pay for the services that the healthcare provider plans to provide for you? Under Medicare Part B, many people are not aware that you could receive from the provider a document known as an **Advance Beneficiary Notice of Noncoverage (ABN)**. Your provider would provide you this form when they realize that Medicare may not pay for the planned services. You will be asked to sign this form to indicate that you understand that the services may not be covered by Medicare. On the form the provider must furnish the estimated charge for the service. If Medicare does not pay for the services, you will be 100-percent responsible for paying the total charge for the services at market rate. It is important that you indicate on the ABN that you want the physician provider to submit a claim for payment to Medicare.

A. Notifier:

B. Patient Name: **C. Identification Number:**

Advance Beneficiary Notice of Noncoverage (ABN)

NOTE: If Medicare doesn't pay for **D.** ____________ below, you may have to pay.

Medicare does not pay for everything, even some care that you or your health care provider have good reason to think you need. We expect Medicare may not pay for the **D.** ____________ below.

D.	E. Reason Medicare May Not Pay:	F. Estimated Cost

WHAT YOU NEED TO DO NOW:

- Read this notice, so you can make an informed decision about your care.
- Ask us any questions that you may have after you finish reading.
- Choose an option below about whether to receive the **D.** ____________ listed above.
  Note: If you choose Option 1 or 2, we may help you to use any other insurance that you might have, but Medicare cannot require us to do this.

G. OPTIONS: Check only one box. We cannot choose a box for you.

☐ **OPTION 1.** I want the **D.** ____________ listed above. You may ask to be paid now, but I also want Medicare billed for an official decision on payment, which is sent to me on a Medicare Summary Notice (MSN). I understand that if Medicare doesn't pay, I am responsible for payment, but **I can appeal to Medicare** by following the directions on the MSN. If Medicare does pay, you will refund any payments I made to you, less co-pays or deductibles.

☐ **OPTION 2.** I want the **D.** ____________ listed above, but do not bill Medicare. You may ask to be paid now as I am responsible for payment. **I cannot appeal if Medicare is not billed.**

☐ **OPTION 3.** I don't want the **D.** ____________ listed above. I understand with this choice I am **not** responsible for payment, and **I cannot appeal to see if Medicare would pay.**

H. Additional Information:

This notice gives our opinion, not an official Medicare decision. If you have other questions on this notice or Medicare billing, call **1-800-MEDICARE** (1-800-633-4227/**TTY:** 1-877-486-2048). Signing below means that you have received and understand this notice. You also receive a copy.

I. Signature:	J. Date:

According to the Paperwork Reduction Act of 1995, no persons are required to respond to a collection of information unless it displays a valid OMB control number. The valid OMB control number for this information collection is 0938-0566. The time required to complete this information collection is estimated to average 7 minutes per response, including the time to review instructions, search existing data resources, gather the data needed, and complete and review the information collection. If you have comments concerning the accuracy of the time estimate or suggestions for improving this form, please write to: CMS, 7500 Security Boulevard, Attn: PRA Reports Clearance Officer, Baltimore, Maryland 21244-1850.

Form CMS-R-131 (03/11) Form Approved OMB No. 0938-0566

If you do not understand the intent of this form or the issues related to giving this form, ask lots of questions. The healthcare provider is required to give you a copy of this ABN form. It is important that you keep it and compare it to the Medicare Explanation of Benefits Form and any bill that you receive from the provider.

If you receive a notice from Medicare that the service has not been paid, you have the right to request an appeal of the initial decision. The patient can submit an appeal or the provider can submit an appeal on behalf of the patient. However, when you request the provider to submit an appeal, it is important that you obtain copies of the documents that the provider has submitted to Medicare to ensure that the provider has completed the appeal process within the timelines outlined in the Medicare Summary Notice. You are at a substantial disadvantage. In many cases, the healthcare provider may have a disincentive to have the Medicare appeal be successful. If the appeal is unsuccessful, the provider would likely be billing you directly at a rate that is far higher than the amount for which Medicare would reimburse them.

MEDICARE PART D (PRESCRIPTION DRUG COVERAGE)

The third level of services covered under Original Medicare, Medicare Part D, is the prescription drug plan.

You obtain such prescription drug plan coverage from a certified Medicare Part D prescription drug insurance program. As with Medicare Part B, you need to make the decision to enroll in the Medicare prescription drug program at the initial time when you turn 65 and do not have a prescription drug program by any other insurance company provider. If you delay in obtaining a prescription drug plan and then decide to enroll at a later time, you will pay a higher premium for Medicare Part D.

The prescription drug plans have multiple options that you can pick from. You need to be sure that all current prescription drugs that you are taking are covered under the prescription drug plan that you are purchasing. The so-called "doughnut hole deductible" (the coverage gap) under the prescription drug plan is slowly decreasing each year. Nonetheless, the coverage gap may still cost you more than $2,000 per year out-of-pocket.

MEDICARE PART C (MEDICARE ADVANTAGE PLANS)

In addition to the Original Medicare program, the Medicare system provides an option known as Medicare Part C, which is the Medicare Advantage Insurance Plans. Medicare Part C consists of managed care plans sold by insurance companies *in place of* Original Medicare. You make this decision either at the time you turn 65, or you can make the change during the open enrollment period which usually occurs between October and December of each year.

Medicare Advantage Plans are offered by private companies, and they are often set up like a Health Maintenance Organization (HMO). Thus, you are agreeing to get the Medicare Part A and B services through healthcare providers within that particular network—rather than through Original Medicare—and you need permission to get coverage outside of the network. It's imperative that you make sure that the physicians, hospitals, and healthcare providers you normally go to have a contract with the specific Medicare Advantage Plan you are considering.

Although you may go to great lengths to ensure your providers participate in the Advantage Plan you've selected, it is possible that, at any time after you enroll, your physicians and your hospital may decide to terminate their contract with the Medicare Advantage Plan. This is a hidden issue that you need to consider when deciding whether to enroll in a Medicare Advantage Plan or an Original Medicare program. Also, if you travel outside of your home area or stay outside of your state in the wintertime, it's possible that your physicians or hospitals in the other state would not have a contract with your Medicare Advantage Plan and you would not receive any benefits. This is a huge risk!

Please note that when you make the initial decision to sign up with a Medicare Advantage Plan, and you subsequently find out your doctors have terminated their contract with that particular plan, it is not possible for you to routinely change from a Medicare Advantage Plan to Original Medicare except during the annual enrollment period of each year. In addition, when you attempt to make the change, not all Medicare Supplement Plans will accept you because of your preexisting conditions. The very first time you enroll for Medicare all insurance companies who market Medicare Supplements must accept you, regardless of your preexisting conditions. You only get one bite of the apple on this privilege. There are hidden risks to choosing a lower-cost Medicare Advantage Plan.

Rick's Thoughts: Medicare Supplement vs. Advantage Plan . . .

Let's look at the differences between a supplement to Original Medicare versus a Medicare Advantage Insurance Plan. I tell clients to ask themselves this question: "Will your Medicare Supplement be accepted by Mayo Clinic in Rochester, Minnesota?" Mayo Clinic has on their website that they will bill you and your

Medicare Advantage Plan, but they make no assurances that your Medicare Advantage Plan will cover the cost. They make that disclaimer because a Medicare Advantage Plan is often set up like an HMO, and to go to Mayo (outside of the network), you will need permission from the network. You'll need to find out how many times your Medicare Advantage network has approved people getting a second opinion at Mayo. On the other hand, Original Medicare with a Medicare Supplement may still have deductible issues for you, depending on what kind of Medicare Supplement you have purchased. As of this writing, Mayo Clinic does accept Medicare with Medicare Supplements, with you being responsible for the deductible.

Nationwide, approximately 50 percent of Medicare recipients are now purchasing a Medicare Advantage Plan. One of the biggest reasons Medicare Advantage Plans sell is their monthly cost savings. However, there is really no standard way to compare Advantage Plans and Supplement Plans because coverage varies by insurance carrier and insurance plan.

Each individual policy stands on its own, and you must be able to understand what coverage you have purchased.

Admittedly, your Medicare Advantage Plan may even cover more things than Original Medicare. I have seen Medicare Advantage Plans that cover dental and vision and even provide you with a free or discounted membership at a health club. Those are not things covered by Original Medicare. But again, with the HMO-type coverage, you must use the in-network doctors and other healthcare providers. That limits you in getting a second opinion or specialty care because Medicare Advantage Plans are not accepted everywhere.

You also need to be concerned about high deductibles. Deductibles will vary depending on which plan you purchase, but you can make no generalizations. You must also know what kind of co-pays you will be subject to. Again, it's a dollars-and-cents computation, but for my clients the big question often is whether they want to have Mayo Clinic or Cleveland Clinic as a second opinion option. If you do, you should supplement Original Medicare with a Medicare Supplement, and our recommendation is that you purchase a Plan F. A Plan F for Blue Cross Blue Shield is the same Plan F that's provided by every other Medicare Supplement insurance company. Most clients make the decision based on service and cost.

In summary, it is critical that anyone making decisions with regards to their Medicare coverage know what they are receiving and be on top of changes in the Medicare program. A great source of information regarding the Medicare program can be found on the Medicare webpage at www.medicare.gov.

It's easy to imagine how medical expenses can leech away the savings you intended for your retirement. By being aware of certain medical expenses and choosing the plan that works for you and your situation, you will be better able to protect and utilize your funds.

Chapter 5

A WEEKEND AWAY

A CHILDREN'S STORY TO SIMPLY EXPLAIN ESTATE PLANNING WITH TRUSTS

Let's start with a little story about a couple going away for a weekend.

Before they go, they decide who will be the best person to take care of their most prized possessions—their children. They contact the best babysitter they know. She has good judgment, is very responsible, and cares deeply about the children. The couple can trust her to take charge of the situation and act according to their wishes and values.

Before leaving, they compile detailed instructions for the sitter . . .

. . . to remind her who should get what, and when.

She reviews the information before the couple leaves to make sure she understands everything, raising any questions or suggestions.

As they say their goodbyes, the couple has the peace of mind that comes with knowing . . .

. . . that everything is in order and their children are in capable hands.

They can really enjoy their weekend away!

Nice story, right? Of course you see the analogy between preparing for a weekend away and preparing to pass on your estate to heirs.

- The babysitter represents the person or persons you select to oversee your financial, property, and healthcare decisions if you become incapacitated or after you pass away.

- The list of instructions represents your estate documents—powers of attorney, wills and/or trusts, etc.—which detail how (and in some cases when) you want your assets distributed, and under whose guidance.

- The peace of mind—well, you've already figured that out. It comes from knowing that you've made important decisions ahead of time so your loved ones won't be burdened by probate, unfinished business, or unanswered questions after your death.

Rick on Estate Planning . . .

Even when individuals work hard their entire lives to accumulate wealth and provide for their families, all of their hard work could come to an end in an instant if they fail to properly plan. And certainly, people lose the ability to put a good, solid estate plan in place if they fail to make arrangements prior to death or incapacity.

Estate planning can really be considered lifetime planning. It should focus on planning for life, as well as for death. This includes not only the life of the individual, but also the lives of family, loved ones, and their heirs. Thus, this type of planning will involve not just financial and tax matters, but also making sure that loved ones will be secure.

Wills and Trusts: The Basics

What happens to an estate upon death—and what can essentially determine the safety of one's assets—will depend in large part on what kind of plan the decedent had in place at the time of their passing.

If one dies without having a will, then they die "intestate." And, whether they have a will or not, their estate will likely go through the probate process. During probate several things happen, including:

- A petition is filed
- The death notice is published
- A hearing is held to validate the will
- Assets are frozen for inventory
- The executor pays debts, taxes, or fees
- The executor files the tax returns
- Assets are distributed
- The estate is closed

If one's estate goes through the probate process, it can essentially take anywhere from nine months to two years to complete. In addition, probate fees are set by state statute and can consume up to 6 percent of the individual's entire estate. And, if the estate goes through probate, the entire proceeding will become public knowledge.

Having a will is certainly a good start in helping to keep assets safe. With a will, retitling of assets won't be necessary, and the decedent's creditors will have only a limited amount of time to make any claims against the estate. In addition, if there are any minor or special needs children involved, a will can provide for the appointment of a guardian.

But there are definite disadvantages if a will is used as the only type of estate planning. Wills are only effective at the time of an individual's death; they offer no opportunity to plan for incapacity. In addition, a will can quickly become outdated, so unless the individual regularly updates it, there could be some real issues upon death. Also, having just a will in place without any other planning documents will still require the estate to go through the probate process.

It is an unending goal of most people to minimize taxes as much as they possibly can and to preserve wealth for themselves and their loved ones. Certainly, that goal comes into view even more clearly when it comes to estate planning.

There are some good reasons for this. Federal estate taxes can get even higher than personal income taxes, with rates as high as 35 percent. When this is combined with inheritance taxes levied by many states, estate tax rates could get to 46 percent or even higher.

Uncle Sam created uniform tax rates for both gift and estate transfers of assets. But, since 2002, Congress has set different tax credits for gifts and estate taxes. For example, the estate tax credit allows every American to pass a specific amount of assets tax-free to their heirs. And, unlike the $1 million gift tax credit that must be used during an individual's lifetime, the estate tax credit is allowed to be used after death when distributing the assets in the estate.

With the passage of the Taxpayer Relief Act of 1997, the estate tax credit gradually increased. However, for the year 2010, there was a full repeal of the estate and gift tax. And with this, people were unsure as to what would happen after 2010.

With President Obama's signing of the Tax Relief, Unemployment Insurance Reauthorization, and Job Creation Act of 2010, federal estate taxes were restored—but not to their original 2002 levels.

Year	Maximum Estate Tax Credit	Maximum Gift Tax Credit	Maximum Unified Rate
2002	$1 million	$1 million	50%
2003	$1 million	$1 million	49%
2004	$1.5 million	$1 million	48%
2005	$1.5 million	$1 million	47%
2006	$2 million	$1 million	46%
2007	$2 million	$1 million	45%
2008	$2 million	$1 million	45%
2009	$3.5 million	$1 million	45%
2010	Repealed	$1 million	35%
2011	$5 million	$1 million	35%
2012	$5.12 million	$5.12 million	35%
2013	$5.25 million	$5.25 million	40%
2014	$5.34 million	$5.34 million	40%
2015	$5.43 million	$5.43 million	40%

Estate taxes are due to the IRS within nine months of the decedent's date of death. Because of this, oftentimes loved ones are forced to sell assets and other belongings in order to pay this tax bill. Unfortunately, in many cases the assets that are sold are let go for far below market value.

There are planning strategies that will not only save and protect assets, but can also allow much more control over where those assets go and how they are utilized. While estate taxes can never completely be eliminated, they can effectively be reduced with the use of different types of trusts.

Zach on Powers of Attorney . . .

As estate planning attorneys, we often get the "we need wills" phone call. This is generally prompted by one of two scenarios. First, a couple is getting on a plane without their kids for the first time since having children. They suddenly realize that they have not made plans to name guardians of their children or a trustee to manage what they would leave behind if the plane goes down. They may not know the legal terminology of "guardian of the person" and "guardian of the estate," or that there is a Trust for Minors Act and they need to set up a trust in accordance with this act. They do know, perhaps for the first time, that they need to plan for the possibility that they could die! You can't believe how "last minute" this call can come. It may be Tuesday when they call, and they tell me they need the wills by Friday because their plane leaves Saturday morning. Nothing like planning ahead!

The second circumstance that often prompts this call is when people receive news that someone they know who is their age or younger has unexpectedly passed away. It might be the first time they've considered that they're not going to live forever. These callers don't feel so urgent to come in, and sometimes they even fail to follow through when the shock of this unexpected death passes.

When we get the "we need wills" call, our response is always the same: they certainly need an estate plan, and especially if they have minor children, they need to address guardianship and trustee issues. For the most part, however, wills are about distributing their "stuff" when they die—and normally we would likely recommend a trust or trusts, depending on the situation, rather than a will. We tell people that what they really need—as much if not more than a will—is powers of attorney. Everyone over the age of 18 needs powers of attorney.

Powers of attorney are about you and how you are cared for when you are living but not able to make decisions for yourself. These documents come into play when someone becomes disabled as result of a disease, an accident, or some other type of tragedy. They allow a person (the principal) to appoint another person (the agent) to be their intercessor, their decision maker when the principal can no longer make his/her own decisions. Powers of attorney should be an essential part of every estate plan. If a person becomes unable to make decisions and no powers of attorney are in place, a court action called a "guardianship" is necessary: the person becomes a ward of the court and a guardian is appointed. Any decisions to be made by the guardian with regards to healthcare or finances must be presented to and approved by the court.

We often get phone calls at our office where the daughter (or son) is telling us that her mother has had a stroke and needs to go to the nursing home. The daughter says, "I am my mother's executor." To which we must reply, "Your mother is not dead, so you are not the executor yet." (Of course, we don't say it as bluntly as that!) The daughter needs a power of attorney for her mother for both healthcare and property. Hopefully, her mother is still mentally competent and able to execute a power of attorney.

The Terri Schiavo case (1990–2005) made the country strikingly aware of the problems presented when no power of attorney has been executed to state the person's wishes regarding life-sustaining issues and to appoint an agent to carry out those end of life decisions. Many people believed the husband should have had the power to end her life, and many others believed that her parents should have been allowed to keep her alive and care for her. Many promoted her right to die, and many advocated for the value of her life. No matter what opinion you held, you probably held an opinion. Terri Schiavo's plight made the entire country aware of the need for individuals to have powers of attorney for healthcare decision-making in place.

What Are "Powerful Powers of Attorney" for Healthcare?

The healthcare power of attorney appoints an agent and allows that agent to talk to your doctors, get your medical records, get a second opinion, or consult on your life support wishes, to name a few of the major areas in which they can act on your behalf. You can designate your agent to withhold or withdraw life support under certain circumstances. We start with the basics of our statutory forms and then customize them for each individual client and also for specific elder law issues that need to be addressed. Our powers of attorney for healthcare discuss particular life support measures that a person may want to consider, such as feeding tubes, ventilators, and hydration. We also discuss life-sustaining measures in the event of advanced dementia. Your healthcare power of attorney may address your wishes with regards to organ donation. It can state your intentions regarding disposition of your body after death, including autopsies, cremation, or other instructions. (Here's a tip: Don't put burial instructions in your will. That document often does not come out until after the burial is completed. Oops!)

What Are "Powerful Powers of Attorney" for Property?

The property power of attorney or "durable" power of attorney appoints an agent and gives that agent certain powers to manage their financial affairs. In Illinois and many other states, these documents are statutory (set out in state law as a form) and can be obtained online or in many office supply stores. However, do not assume this ease of access means ease of completion. There are many issues to be considered when completing the documents—personal and legal matters that should be discussed with someone who knows the right questions to ask and who possesses the right understanding of the powers that will be or can be granted under these documents.

In Illinois, general powers to manage financial affairs are specifically listed. The specific list of powers can be customized to either limit or expand the powers. We add powers to the list based on our experience with over 5,000 senior clients. It is important to have these powers explained to you by legal counsel, since the "instructions" can be confusing and there are many important powers with regard to gifting, trust management, changing beneficiaries, and other broad powers that must be explored and explained.

I often see forms that have been completed incorrectly, choices left blank, multiple choices checked where there should only be one, improper witnesses (cannot be "interested parties" and certainly cannot be the named agents), and many other errors and omissions. Another tip: If possible, always list back-up agents. If your primary agent cannot serve due to death, incapacity or unwillingness to serve, you want to make sure that you have listed back-up agents. If the principal (you) becomes incapacitated and then the agent dies with no back-up agents listed, the principal (you again) requires a guardianship action to appoint someone to be the guardian of the person and estate. You literally become a ward of the court.

WILLS DO NOT PREVENT PROBATE

Probate is the long and expensive courtroom process of getting a will approved by a judge. Contrary to what many people believe, wills do NOT avoid probate. Somewhere along the way, someone probably told you that if you die without a will, your estate goes through probate. This is true. However, people tend to conversely assume that if you die with a will, your estate *will not* go through probate. This is *false.*

Some attorneys tell their clients that they don't need a trust and that they should just do a "simple will" or "sweetheart wills." The simple will for the individual passes his assets to his named beneficiary and nominates an executor. "Sweetheart wills" refer to wills where the husband leaves everything to his wife and the wife leaves everything to her husband—and then the surviving spouse leaves the assets to the children or other named beneficiary.

Why would an attorney recommend a document that will take you through probate when he could do a trust that would avoid probate? Perhaps because some attorneys think of trust planning as having to do with avoiding inheritance (or death) taxes on the estate. Also, the truth is that if your attorney gives you a will (and graciously offers to keep the originals in his safety deposit box), he is almost guaranteed that he will get your future business whenever you want to make changes to that will, and he will often make a large fee when your family comes back to him to probate your will.

Wills are "death planning." Remember the call Zach told you about where the daughter said she was her mother's "executor," and we had to break it to her that she has no power under this document until her mother dies? The truth is, even if her mother was deceased, the daughter would not be the executor until she is appointed by the court. A "named executor" is simply nominated in the will and must petition the court to be appointed the executor, and they must have "letters of office" to act. The point is that the "testator" must die for the will to be in force.

Sometimes people ask if they should "file" or "record" their wills. We explain that the will has no power until the death of the testator, and that is why it can be changed with a codicil (a document changing a part of the will)—or it can be completely redone, in which case the old one is revoked. Almost all wills begin by saying, "I revoke any prior will or codicil . . ." If there are two wills in existence at the time of a person's death, and both are "valid" wills (which means that they meet all the criteria required by state law, such as two witnesses and a notary public), the court will presume that it is the most recent one that dictates, even if it failed to state that any prior will is revoked.

When you do an estate plan that has a trust, you also get a companion will. However, it is not a "simple will" or a "sweetheart will." It is what is referred to as a "pour-over will." This will states that the person has a trust, and in the event that he has assets at the time of his death that are in the person's name and not in the trust, the person wishes the executor to "pour these assets over" into the trust.

NOT ALL TRUSTS ARE ALIKE

Many times, we get a call from an adult child who has just been told that his or her elderly parent needs long-term care in a facility. The child will tell us, "My mom has a trust, so everything is protected." We have to ask, "Is it a revocable living trust?" The answer often comes back quickly, "Yes." The person on the other end of the phone is thinking that all is well. We have to then inform them that the trust is completely available to be spent down on care for the parent. Sometimes, the child is confused: "But doesn't the trust protect the assets?" Sometimes the child is angry: "The lawyer said this would protect Mom's assets!" Sometimes we hear denial: "No, that just can't be right."

The problem is that *not all trusts are alike.* When you hear the word "trust," you think it sounds like a good word. What the parent has in this case is what we refer to as "the open box." This means that at any time the trustmaker can reach into the open box (the trust), take out money, and spend it on whatever they want. But if *they* can reach into the open box and spend the income and assets, so can *creditors* (which would include a long-term care facility). All the assets are available for medical expenses of the person who created the trust and has had control of the trust.

Some trusts are referred to as "revocable living trusts," meaning they can be revoked or amended. The money in them can be used for the trustmaker's **h**ealthcare costs, **e**ducation costs, **m**aintenance expenses, and **s**upport; we call this the "HEMS" standard.

People most commonly are told they should get a trust to avoid probate. Revocable living trusts may *avoid probate* if properly funded, but they are *not asset-protection trusts.*

Does the parent have a trust? Yes. Will they avoid probate at death? It depends. Are the assets in the trust protected against being spent down on care? No. That would be an entirely different type of trust. In general, trusts that protect assets are referred to as "irrevocable trusts," and even these trusts are not all the same.

Let's look at trust basics, and then we will look at different trusts and the purposes and goals of each.

TRUST BASICS

Some trusts are "revocable," and that sounds non-threatening. Some trusts are "irrevocable," and that sounds scary. But even within those two basic categories, there can be many types of trusts that serve different purposes and help clients achieve certain goals.

Now let's look at the "players":

- First, you have the **trustmaker,** sometimes called the "grantor." The trustmaker is one of the individuals who will sign the trust. You can have more than one trustmaker.

- Next, there is the **trustee**. The trustee is the "manager" of the trust. The trustmaker can also be the trustee. You can have more than one trustee—"co-trustees." If a trustee can no longer serve, the trustmaker can appoint people to step up into that role. They are called "successor trustees," and you can name several in the order you wish them to substitute when there is a vacancy. The trust contains a list of all of the powers that the trustee has with regard to the trust. The trustee has a fiduciary duty to carry out the trustmaker's instructions. The initial trustee will also sign the trust.

- Finally, you have the **beneficiary** or **beneficiaries.** This is the person, persons, charity or organization that will get the trustmaker's stuff.

One thing to remember about a trust is that it holds assets *during the life* of the trustmaker and *not just at death* like a will. The trustee will be managing assets owned by the trust while the trustmaker is healthy, disabled, *and* deceased. It is not only death planning; it is also life planning.

In our office we have a large variety of trusts because we have clients with a large variety of needs and circumstances.

We don't call our trusts simply "revocable trusts" or "irrevocable trusts." Those two terms lack the specificity that is needed to identify a trust. We try to be explicit with the names so they describe the purpose and goal of each trust. Trusts are complicated in nature and can be designed to meet very precise needs. We want clients to get "trusts they can trust."

INCOME AND ASSET CONTROL TRUSTS (IACT): A LIVING TRUST

This trust is—as we describe it in our office—an open box. The assets you "fund" into this trust and all income produced from those assets are completely available to the trustmaker(s). The trustmaker (owner of the assets placed into the trust) is generally also the trustee (manager of those assets). The trust is for the trustmaker's use for his or her health, education, maintenance, and support (the HEMS standard) while he or she is living. It includes such things as who will manage the trust if the trustmaker becomes disabled and how it should be managed at that time, as well as who should manage the trust when the trustmaker dies and what will happen to all remaining assets in the trust. It can be as simple as this:

John Smith, Trustmaker, creates an Income and Asset Control Trust (IACT). During his lifetime, he has full access to the assets in the trust and any income they produce. When he opens an account in the name of the trust, he uses his own Social Security number and he titles it "The John Smith Trust Dated [whatever day it was signed], John Smith, Trustee." Any interest or gain that the assets in the IACT accrue, John Smith reports on his personal income tax return, and there is no need to do a separate return for the trust. When John dies, his successor trustee, his daughter Mary Smith, reads the instructions, which say: 40 percent to Mary, 40 percent to Tom (his son), and 20 percent to be divided equally among the four grandchildren. Mary, as the successor trustee, must follow those instructions. Because John used our firm, Law ElderLaw, all of his assets are properly titled in the trust, including his bank accounts, investment accounts, stocks, and residence. Mary proceeds to liquidate everything and put the money into the checking account titled in John's IACT, and then she can write checks per John's instructions. No probate, no court costs, no attorney fees (unless Mary wants some help with the trust administration), no lengthy waiting period to distribute assets.

If John had not died but rather become ill, it would be important for John's trust to have stated how he wanted Mary to proceed during his long-term care. Did he want everything used for his care? Maybe he really wanted to stay at home if at all possible. Did he want Mary to seek the counsel of an elder law attorney to pursue some protection planning? If so, John will have given Mary the ability to do such planning in the trust. He will have also given some broad powers in his power of attorney for property. It will be a very good thing that John has a power of attorney for property, as prepared by Law ElderLaw, that built in the necessary planning powers—not just one of those statutory form documents you can buy at the office supply store.

It could be that this trust was used to do some inheritance tax planning as well. It could be that John's wife is living and he is going to pay some assets to her in a marital trust and some to a secondary trust to be held until his wife dies, and then be transferred to children or grandchildren. John's wife would have her own IACT that would mirror his, and again this type of trust planning is used to make sure that both trustmakers are able to keep their inheritance tax credit amount.

For example, in 2009, the credit was $3.5 million. The year 2010 was the "get out of estate tax free" year. However, this was a sunset law and Congress needed to set the bar for 2011. They finally arrived at $5 million. If you leave an estate worth more than that, the federal government will be happy to take about 50 percent of any amount over the $5 million. If a couple has $12 million and they don't do this type of tax planning with the separate IACTs (sometimes referred to as A/B trust planning) and they simply hold everything in joint or they have wills that leave everything to each other, one will end up with the entire $12 million, and when the surviving spouse dies, the government will take approximately 50 percent of $2 million. You can see that the income and asset control trust is a very valuable tool in both simple planning and more complex tax planning.

INCOME AND ASSET CONTROL TRUSTS—SPOUSAL BYPASS

We have a variation of the IACT that we refer to as "spousal bypass." This trust would be used when the trustmaker does not wish to leave his or her assets to the spouse, but rather wishes for the assets to go directly to children or grandchildren (or other family members). We use this in the cases where one spouse is ill and may even be in a nursing home receiving public benefits. The healthy spouse may wish to bypass the ill spouse, knowing that any assets left to the ill spouse will be quickly used up to pay the nursing home. The healthy spouse may instead wish for the assets to pass directly to other family members. The IACT assets and income are used for the trustmaker during his or her lifetime, and when the trustmaker dies, the assets bypass the surviving spouse and pass according to the instructions left by the trustmaker in the trust.

We can include a provision in this trust to create a testamentary trust for the surviving spouse that could be used for "special needs." This testamentary trust would be set up in the will, and it would not interfere with public benefits by pouring back funds to the estate.

WEALTH PROTECTOR TRUSTS (WPT), ALSO KNOWN AS ASSET PROTECTION TRUSTS (APT): THE SEALED BOX

Now we move into the realm of trusts where assets really are protected from future spend-down. This is not the "revocable living trust" that the child *thought* offered protection to the parent's assets if they became disabled and needed nursing home care. This is a trust that actually *does* offer protection to certain assets that the trustmaker wants to make sure are his or her legacy.

This level of planning can provide protection for the trustmaker's assets in a variety of circumstances. The protection can be needed as a result of a serious diagnosis for the trustmaker, as protection for a beneficiary who will be inheriting under the trust, or as protection for future income for a loved one.

In this type of trust (and there are several variations), the person can move assets into a "sealed box" so that whatever is in the box is saved as the person's legacy. Some of the aspects of the trust are indeed "irrevocable" and some are not. There are a number of considerations regarding this protection, and each trust is designed to follow those considerations.

There may be enough assets outside the trust or enough time until the need for care to get through a 60-month window or "look-back" for Medicaid purposes. The funds in this trust are not yet completely "gifted" to the heirs, but will pass to the heirs at the person's death (again outside of the probate process). And, if that person goes to a nursing home *after* the five years from the date the trust was signed and funded, then those assets are "safe." As we mentioned above, there are several variations of this trust. In one variation all assets and income are "safe" and do not go to the trustmaker after funding. In another variation, the trustmaker can retain income produced from the assets in the trust.

One of the wealth protector trusts preserves the step-up in basis for the appreciated assets and keeps the homestead exemption. This is a very specific irrevocable trust with lots of "bells and whistles" to protect assets while creating a "trap door" to get assets out to lifetime beneficiaries. We use this trust to help the trustmaker qualify for such benefits as Veterans Administration "Aid and Attendance" or AABD Medicaid assistance.

In another variation, the person can pass the assets to a trusted child and have that child be the trustmaker. As we mentioned in the section on "Trust Basics," in our office we have a large variety of trusts because we have clients with a large variety of needs and circumstances. We can protect assets from spend-down on long-term care, and we don't want the problems of the children to bump into the protected assets of the parents.

We can also use financial products within trusts to set aside assets in a safe place. The assets can be protected from spend-down by the trustmaker and/or qualify the trustmaker for benefits to create future income for the person, spouse, or child, or to protect the inheritance for (and sometimes *from*) the beneficiary.

The next section will cover trust planning for the beneficiary's protection.

TRUSTS THAT PROTECT THE VULNERABLE, DISABLED, OR SELF-DESTRUCTIVE ADULT CHILD

As we meet with clients it becomes clear to us that many people are concerned about what will happen to their loved ones who are particularly vulnerable. It may be a child who has been disabled either physically or mentally since birth; that child may be living at home or in some type of group home setting. It may be a child with severe learning disabilities who the parents have continued to care for and support while trying to help him or her be as independent as possible. It may be a child that was perfectly healthy at birth and up to adulthood, but in later years developed a disability such as MS, or became disabled as a result of an accident and is now in need of extra care and support. This type of trust can be revocable or irrevocable during the trustmaker's lifetime.

The beneficiary may also be a child that simply "failed to launch." It may be a child that is currently in an abusive relationship. It may be a child that has never been able to, and likely will never be able to, handle money. It may be a child that had (or still has) an addiction. Whatever the reason, these parents see that they have a vulnerable adult child who will need continuing care and support.

It may be that a child has been caring for his or her parent, but now that child is ill and has *become* the estate planning client. We recently met with a daughter who had been battling cancer, and it had become apparent to her that she would lose the battle in the very near future. Her mother was living independently at home, but the daughter had been assisting in her support for quite some time. She wanted to make sure that her mother's special needs were taken care of, but that the money was not left outright to her mother for fear of financial abuse, creditors, predators, and the high cost of a nursing home if that level of care became necessary.

It may be that the client has no children but has a beloved pet and they are concerned that no one will care for the pet after their death. We have had clients who have horses that they are very concerned about what will happen to them at the time of their deaths. We have seen clients run "no kill" shelters and they fear for what will happen when they are gone. Or it might just be Grandma's dog or cat that no one will want when Grandma passes.

We have developed within our firm several trusts that are designed to care for those loved ones that our clients may be leaving behind and whom they see as vulnerable. Those clients understand that they cannot leave money to these individuals outright, since the beneficiaries cannot handle money well and would inevitably be taken advantage of and left unprotected.

These trusts, outlined below, provide peace of mind for the trustmakers that their loved ones will be cared for and not exploited.

TENDER LOVING CARE TRUST (TLC TRUST)

The technical name for this trust is a "supplemental needs trust." This is a trust where the trustmaker creates the trust and funds it either during his or her lifetime or at death. We suggest that the TLC trust be created separately, or stand alone. We have seen many wills and trusts where the person states that at his or her death a trust should be created for a beneficiary. Trusts that are contained inside a will are called "testamentary trusts" and do not begin until the death of the testator. We say those trusts are "trapped inside the will." Why is that a bad thing? In the case of a spouse, it is actually a *requirement* that a "special needs trust" for a spouse be testamentary in order to protect the assets from spend-down on health, education, maintenance, and support (remember the HEMS standard) and to not interfere with the person's public benefits. However, in the case of anyone other than a spouse, there is no need for the trust to be testamentary, and it is actually not the best planning.

If the trust is for a child or any other person with disabilities (not the spouse), it is a "third-party" special needs trust. This means that someone created a trust for another person (again not a spouse) and funded that trust with money that did not belong to the person with disabilities. When you do this, you can say, "The assets in this trust can be used for the person's special needs to supplement and not supplant public benefits."

You decide what happens to any remaining trust assets when the person with disabilities passes away.

If you have the trust created as a stand-alone trust, you can then fund the trust during your lifetime and others can offer assets for the trust or designate assets in their will to pass to this trust as well. Since the trust is already in existence, another person (say a grandparent) would only have to reference this trust in their will. They would not have to create a separate trust inside their will just in case they die while you are still alive with no special needs trust in place (because it is trapped in your will).

LOVE AND PROTECTION TRUST (LPT) AND THE IRA INHERITANCE PROTECTION TRUST

In June, 2014, the United States Supreme Court stated in *Clark v. Rameker, Bankruptcy Trustee*, that after an IRA creator's death, if the beneficiary of the IRA has creditors and/or divorce problems, then all of the inherited IRA may be subject to loss. In addition, in a 2014 Illinois Appellate Court case, *Community Bank of Elmhurst v. Klein*, a creditor's lien was enforced against the interests of a beneficiary son.

Many of our clients fear the possibility that the inheritance that they intend to leave to their children and/or grandchildren will be "blown-out" due to mishandling or vulnerabilities of the inheritor. We use our Love and Protection Trusts and IRA Inheritance Protection Trusts as a tool to stretch-out our client's inheritance for the benefit of their often pension-less loved ones.

Some clients have children that are not legally disabled either physically or mentally. These individuals have not been adjudicated "disabled" by Social Security or by a court—but throughout their lives they have suffered from emotional problems or relationship problems, or they simply have been unable to manage money, or they are vulnerable to manipulation by predators.

When we interview our clients, we have questions on our intake form that read as follows:

- When you think about this child, what is the best keyword to generally describe him/her? *(examples: loving, stubborn, goofy, energetic, disciplined, pensive, happy, troubled, forgetful)*

- When it comes to handling money, what is a keyword that comes to mind when you think of this child? *(examples: reliable, honest, reckless, hole-in-the-pocket)*

This can be very revealing. Parents are generally quite up-front when discussing a child that has physical or mental handicap issues, but it can be difficult for them to bring up the fact that they have a child that is "very loving, but reckless with money." You have a child that you see as troubled, and when it comes to money there seems to be a "hole-in-the-pocket" and you don't even know what they do with their money—and maybe you're afraid to ask.

We can use this trust to provide lifetime income for a child when the parent is concerned about him/her getting a large lump sum. This can create an income stream for the life of the child without the child being able to access the account balance and liquidate it.

We have found that this planning is not necessarily just for children who are reckless with money or easily taken advantage of. This planning can also simply provide a pension for a child. As we have stated, we may need to consider that our children may not have sufficient income in *their* retirement years.

DIGNITY FOR CLIENT TRUST (D4C TRUST)

This trust is very much like the TLC trust mentioned above, with one specific exception: it is funded with the assets of the person with disabilities or with assets from his or her living spouse (not one created by will or "testamentary"). If you create a "special needs trust" with your own assets or create one for your spouse while you are alive, this trust is referred to as "self-settled," and at the death of the person with disabilities, remaining assets are subject to claims by the state of Illinois up to the amount expended on the person through public benefits.

This trust is also referred to as a "pooled trust" and can be used when a person with disabilities who is on public benefits receives an inheritance or a lump sum settlement. A spouse could create such a trust for the disabled spouse with a certain amount of funds during the healthy spouse's lifetime in order to protect that amount of money for the disabled spouse's special needs.

PET EXPENSES TRUST (PET)

This trust is exactly what it sounds like. It is a trust created to provide assets for the care of beloved pets such as horses, birds, dogs, and so on. These animals have been under the trustmaker's care and need to be provided for after the death of the trustmaker. It could even be funds for an animal shelter that the trustmaker wishes to donate to for a specific need. This trust gives peace of mind to the trustmaker that the pet will not be abandoned or euthanized after the death of the trustmaker.

The trust will have specific instructions regarding the care for pet, the person or persons they would prefer provide this care, and how the trust assets should be expended on behalf of the pet.

As you can see, not all trusts are alike. Some trusts are revocable and some are irrevocable, but there is so much more to the planning than meets the eye. Some trusts hold the assets to be managed by the trustee as he or she sees fit, and some trusts work better when coupled with financial products. *It is important for the trusts to be funded.* And it is most important for the trustmaker to be able to trust their legal counsel and for that legal counsel to endeavor to deliver trustworthy trusts.

Chapter 6

THE LAW ELDERLAW PYRAMID OF ESTATE AND ASSET PROTECTION PLANNING

A LEVEL-BY-LEVEL APPROACH TO PLANNING

If you are typical of most people, you have, at best, a very basic concept about what estate planning is and what it can do. Very few people—including attorneys—have a deep understanding of estate planning. Thus, they tend to believe that all estate plans are the same, other than the price. Nothing could be further from the truth.

We want our clients to see their future in a new way. When they come to us, we want to help them to have two realizations, which we call the two "ah-ha" or "light-bulb" moments:

- Estate planning can do more for you and your loved ones than you ever imagined.

- Understanding how healthcare is paid for during the senior years is absolutely critical to protecting you, your survivor spouse, and your loved ones.

The typical view of estate planning is very simplistic and goes like this: "If I die, leave everything to my sweetheart. If my sweetheart is gone, then leave everything equally to my children's checking accounts." Well, maybe you never thought about the money that you leave for your children going directly to their checking accounts, but that is actually one of the big issues we'll cover in this chapter. If you leave everything directly to your children, it does go to their checking accounts, and from there it is subject to be taken by divorce, a manipulative spouse, creditors, and frivolous spending.

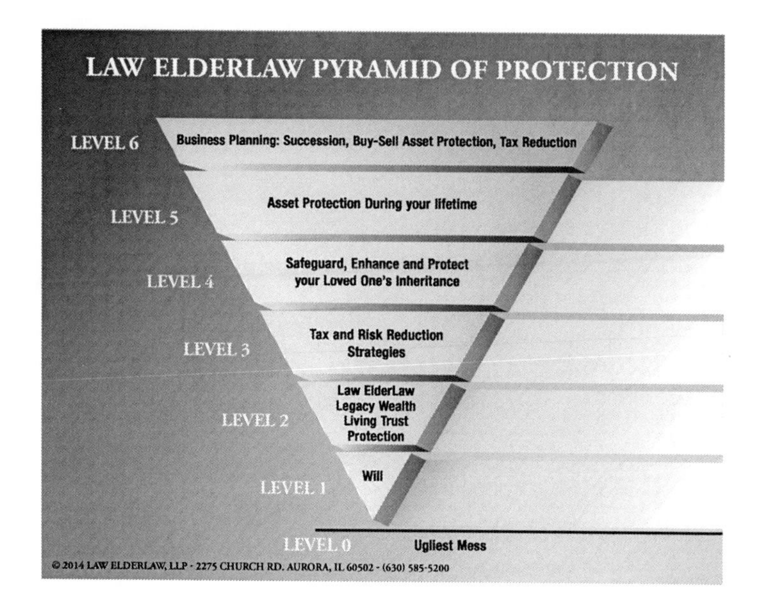

The Law ElderLaw Pyramid of Estate Planning and Protection is designed to help you have those two ah-ha moments. So let's begin.

LEVEL 0: THE UGLIEST MESS

Level zero is actually below the pyramid. Level zero is when people do nothing. When you do nothing, typically things are quite disorganized. Perhaps you put the name of one child on one checking account, the name of another child on a CD, the name of another child on a life insurance policy, and somehow it's all supposed to work out. But when you don't do any comprehensive planning, you often wind up with the ugliest mess. When clients have left their assets to be divided either by designated beneficiary forms or the plan left by the state of Illinois, many times there's going to be a courtroom and a judge involved in straightening everything out.

In addition, during your lifetime you are left exposed to needing a courtroom and a judge to make decisions about your life in the event that you become suddenly disabled by a stroke, a heart attack, or an accident. If you are unable to make decisions for yourself, then an attorney will need to go to court to petition that a judge order someone to make decisions for you. When you're at level zero, you stand a high risk of needing what we call "living probate" during your life, and "post-death probate" to deal with your assets once you're gone.

The other thing about level zero is that if you don't make a plan for distribution, the state of Illinois has a plan for you. It's expensive, a hassle, and painful for loved ones. If you are not comfortable with that plan, then let's move on to level one.

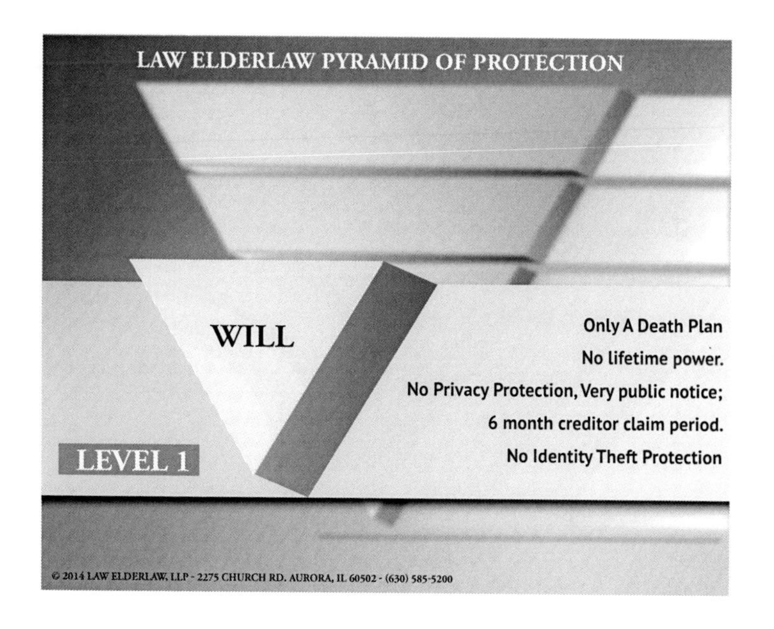

LEVEL 1: WILL

Level one is the second most popular plan. Level one is a will. A will can be created on a piece of paper where you write down how you want things distributed at the end of your life, and you get two witnesses to sign after you sign it. If you want to get fancy, you can also add a notary after those two witnesses, but the notary is extra. If you do a simple will, you have gone beyond level zero in that you have made a plan for yourself. However, after you die, someone has to be appointed as the executor, and that requires going to court. In fact, we have a state law that states that your executor must file your will within 30 days of your death, and after that everything becomes very public.

The whole concept of probate revolves around proving that the will is valid, giving an opportunity for creditors to file their claims against your assets, and allowing any disagreements among your heirs to have a courtroom to share their woes. A will is an ancient form of distribution of your assets, and it requires a six-month claim period, an advertisement in the paper for someone to come and file a claim, and then communication with all heirs to let them know that they have an opportunity to voice their concerns prior to the ultimate distribution. In addition, this is all very public and anyone—not just an attorney or a person from the court—has access to all of your personal information, which is easily readable and can be copied. A will acts like a compass that points toward the closest courthouse, and with a will or with doing nothing you can expect that your family members will be spending time and money before anything is distributed to them.

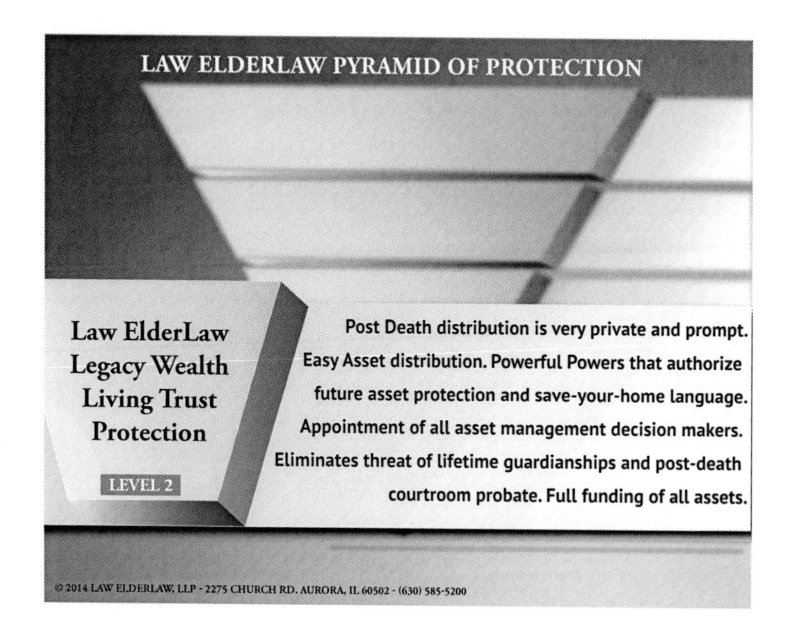

LEVEL 2: LEGACY WEALTH LIVING TRUST PROTECTION

Level two is a much-preferred way of handling your estate during your life and during distribution. Here at Law ElderLaw we call level two the Legacy Wealth Living Trust Protection. When we get to this particular level, we are providing our clients a great tool to avoid probate in a way that is customized to their values and allows them to maintain privacy and control, and avoid courtroom involvement. Living trusts are excellent tools and are considered to be the core component of modern estate planning. We, as experienced estate planners, draft living trusts for our clients to fulfill their wishes regarding the distribution of their assets. Living trusts allow them to have control during their lifetime and to appoint appropriate successors after they're gone.

In addition, we coordinate their living trusts with all other necessary documents to protect them. The Legacy Wealth Living Trust Protection package always includes healthcare powers of attorney and financial powers of attorney, as well as ancillary documents such as the trust certifications and appropriate affidavits. We work to give our clients comprehensive trusts that enable them to avoid living probate. With a well-drafted trust that is fully funded with assets, our clients can know that everything has been done that needs to be done to avoid courtrooms.

Funding is the act of transferring a client's assets into the appropriate trust or trusts. In chapter 5 we illustrated how a trust is like a box into which you put the valuable and nourishing assets to be used by you or your beneficiaries. The trust really doesn't work if you haven't put those important things into the box. We see many trusts created by other attorneys or do-it-yourselfers that, while the language may be sufficient to transfer assets from one generation to the next, misses a key component: the actual correct funding of the trust. We often say that the word funding has the letters *f*, *u*, *n* in it, but there is nothing fun about funding. Funding is an activity to be done by a person who is highly detailed and analytical—a person who is trained to persevere and work with banks, insurance companies, brokerage houses, financial institutions, the United States government, and a host of other entities that control assets owned by our clients.

In our office, we have full-time staff dedicated to working on funding the trust so that our clients' wishes are realized after their passing, and so that we can sit down with clients during trust administration and many times say to them, "Well there's almost nothing that you need us for." That is the ultimate compliment to good trust planning—that after your death things can be handled with dignity, privacy, and promptness.

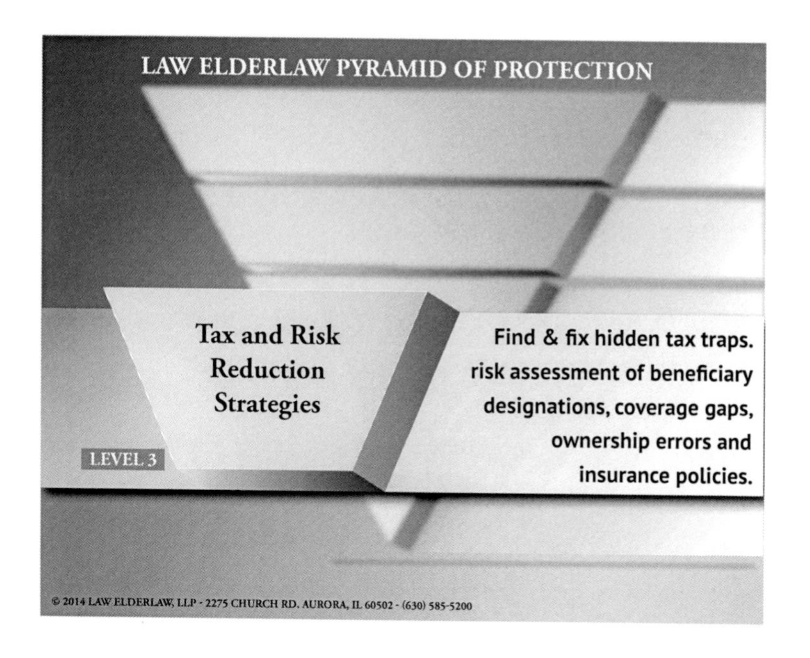

LEVEL 3: TAX AND RISK REDUCTION STRATEGIES

In our office, when we're going through the trust creation and funding process, part of our job is to find and fix hidden traps. Sometimes those hidden traps are tax traps. Other times we want to do a risk assessment regarding how you have set up your prior transfer documents to make sure that everything is coordinated with your estate plan. Many times we find that our clients intend that their assets be passed in one particular way, but when we review their designated beneficiary forms, we find that those forms are filled out quite differently than our clients remember.

Another thing that comes up during the funding process is the discovery of errors or misunderstandings regarding the ownership and titling of real estate. Proper handling of real estate is so important to us that we always request that a title search be done of your real estate to ensure that, when we fund your trusts, the real estate is being properly retitled from its current owners to the trust as the owner.

Lastly, this is a great moment to review life insurance and other insurances to ensure that there are no gaps in coverage, which cause great risk for our clients. We often ask our clients if they wish to have a risk assessment review for some of the common issues that arise during this process. In many cases, we coordinate with our network of experts to have them review each one of our clients' unique circumstances.

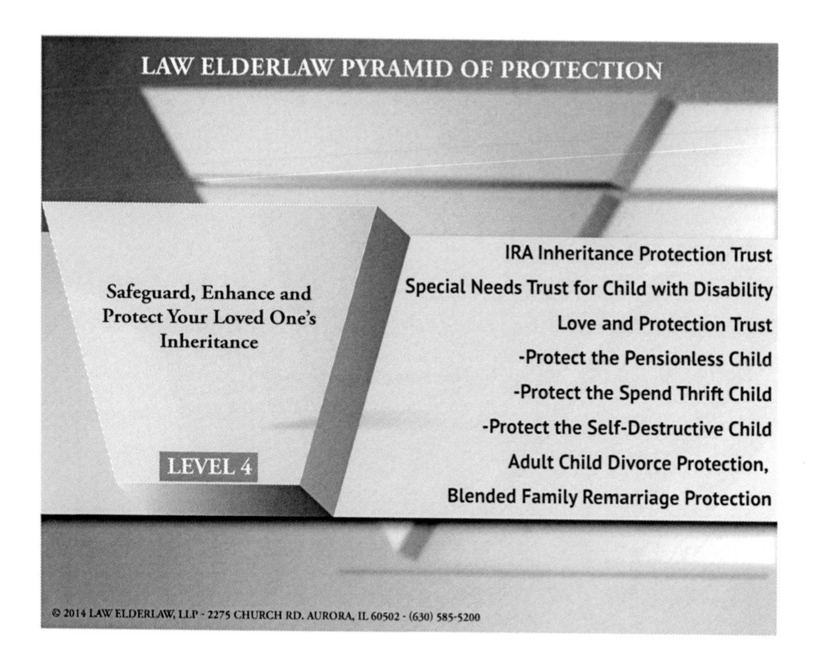

LEVEL 4: SAFEGUARD, ENHANCE, AND PROTECT YOUR LOVED ONE'S INHERITANCE

This level of planning is the number one reason that clients engage us to represent them in their estate planning. There are many, many things that need to be done to ensure that the distribution of the assets is properly handled after your death. In some family situations, there are issues related to possible remarriage. When women die before their male spouse, it is very common that men get remarried within a relatively short period of time. Clients who are concerned about protecting their children's inheritance often want special language built into the estate plan to ensure that, after the death of the first wife, the assets the husband and wife have acquired together will not be lost due to the surviving husband dying and leaving everything to his new wife and her children. Of course, the same is true the other way around.

Many couples have a blended marriage. She may have children from a prior marriage, he may have children from a prior marriage, and they may have children together. This creates a complex situation that requires very careful estate planning. We have seen many situations dealing with aging clients where these kinds of problems have never been worked out. It's especially ugly when one spouse dies and the surviving spouse and her children are busily defending themselves from attacks by his children who want their share of the estate now.

This kind of planning needs to be worked out when people are healthy and capable and can make the right decision based on their family's facts and circumstances. It's also critically important for the surviving spouse to have clarity about what his or her deceased spouse actually wanted to have happen with the estate after they were gone. Men die before women of the same age 80 percent of the time. This leaves the surviving widow to deal with his children who in many cases can be angry and aggressive regarding their "fair share" of the estate. Don't let this happen in your family.

Other marriage issues actually focus on your beneficiary generation. If you do nothing except designate your child as a beneficiary, then you are guaranteeing that your estate is going directly to your child's checking account. In many situations, that checking account is a marital checking account. In some states, as soon as those assets hit that checking account, your son-in-law or daughter-in-law may have access to 100 percent of what you have left to your child. That checking account has absolutely no asset protection from your adult child's spouse, divorce, or creditors.

A recent case brings this to the forefront. Recently in Illinois there was an appellate court case with the title of *Community Bank of Elmhurst v. Klein*. This case was decided in DuPage County in 2014 and then affirmed by the Illinois Appellate Court. The fact pattern is this: Ruth Klein died and left money to her son George. Unfortunately George had an existing creditor, the Community Bank of Elmhurst. As soon as money was distributed from the deceased mother's estate directly to George, the Community Bank of Elmhurst liened $72,690.97. If mom had known that she could create an asset protection trust to put a protective wrapper around the estate she was leaving for George, she probably would have done that. Of course she would have had to pay for a more expensive estate plan to provide that kind of asset protection, but she would not have even paid 10 percent of the loss of $72,690.

We work with clients to help them put protective wrappers around the monies that they're leaving for the next generation so that the assets do not go directly to the child's checking account. Many of our clients want to give their adult children a better form of estate planning so they will be protected and so their children will be able to stretch out the benefits of the estate. Our clients know that most of their adult children are part of the pension-less generation. Nonetheless, *The Wall Street Journal* has reported that most inheritances are completely spent within 18 months. We work with our clients to provide solutions that keep their inheritance from being squandered by the inheritors, their creditors, or their spouses.

Love and protection trust planning is a key part of level four. The primary reasons for creating a trust that will receive your inheritance for the benefit of your loved one is to do the following:

- Protect the pension-less child by providing them with a reasonable and orderly payout of the inheritance over time.

- Protect the spendthrift child who would otherwise dissipate the inheritance in a short amount of time.

- Protect the self-destructive child who is burdened with addictions to drugs, alcohol, gambling, and other life destroying behaviors.

- Protect the adult child who has or may experience divorce.

Three to five percent of our clients have children or grandchildren who have had a disability since birth. Those children with special needs rarely have the ability to be self-supporting by finding a place within the work environment; they must be protected. Our clients often wish to provide dignity funds to enable a child or grandchild with special needs to enjoy a life beyond what the government would provide. A child with special needs is usually qualified for Supplemental Security Income (SSI) through the Social Security Administration. These days, that check is no more than about $700 per month. In addition, a child with special needs also must stay qualified for SSI by having almost no assets and an extremely low income from other sources.

This creates a unique dilemma. The SSI is not an income that anyone could live on. Nonetheless, it's the foundation for all the rest of the governmental framework for assistance. Please note that the state of Illinois is classified as the 50th lowest provider of benefits to persons with special needs. So to provide a child with special needs with money for vacations, special therapies, education, music, electronics, fashion glasses, clothing, etc., one creates a special needs trust. It's the legal way to preserve public benefits, including Medicaid, and pay for retaining the dignity and improving the life of a child or grandchild that you love.

Lastly, many of our clients have an IRA or other retirement-qualified funds expected to outlive both themselves and their spouse. Typically a person signs a designated beneficiary form and lists each of their children or grandchildren to whom their IRA will be distributed. But as you think about that in light of this chapter, now you realize that you're aiming directly at your child's checking account. In June of 2014, the Supreme Court of the United States made a very important decision in a case entitled *Clark v. Rameker, Bankruptcy Trustee.* In that case, the Supreme Court stated that if you do nothing more than leave your IRA to the next generation's checking account, then those monies and the inherited IRA in total are subject to claim by your child's creditors.

Here are the facts of the case. Ruth Heffron, trust creator, left a $450,000 IRA to her daughter Heidi Heffron-Clark. Six years later, due to the failure of Heidi's husband's business, the two of them filed bankruptcy. As the bankruptcy trustee was going through the assets of Mr. and Mrs. Clark, he claimed that the inherited IRA, which by then was worth about $300,000, was available to the Clark's business creditors for repayment of debt. The Clarks went to court and their attorney argued that those assets that had been accumulated by Heidi's mother were IRA retirement funds, which were protected by the Federal Bankruptcy Code. The United States Supreme Court knew that in different parts of the country there were conflicting decisions on this matter, so it took the case.

The Supreme Court determined that inherited IRA funds in the next generation were not protected from bankruptcy creditors of the beneficiary. The court stated in part, "there is nothing to prevent the beneficiary of an inherited IRA from immediately spending the money on any purpose, whether luxury or frivolous. Therefore since there is nothing that keeps them from immediately spending the money, there is no reason to consider these protected retirement funds under the Bankruptcy Code." What had been decided at that moment was that if you left your IRA or other retirement-qualified funds directly to any of your beneficiaries, they may be lost to creditors, divorce, or rapid spending by the beneficiary.
Many of our clients have spent their entire adult lives accumulating their retirement-qualified funds and IRAs. They have spent their retirement years protecting their IRA from excessive expenditures even by themselves. It

grieves them to imagine that after their death the IRA funds they have spent decades protecting could be immediately spent or taken. To help our clients have peace of mind and to continue protecting what they have worked so hard to earn and save, those clients choose to do a protective wrapper around the stream of income from the IRA. This protection is known as the **IRA Inheritance Protection Trust**. This trust can be written to achieve your values. In the event that you are worried that your beneficiary will squander the IRA rather than stretch out the benefits, we will work with you to help you design an appropriate distribution pattern.

It's important to point out that if you're worried about the assets being blown or 100-percent lost, you do need to recognize that there will be a higher tax cost for your children's generation if you place certain restrictions on their expenditures. This issue can be discussed with you in more detail by our tax attorneys and accountant during the legal design process.

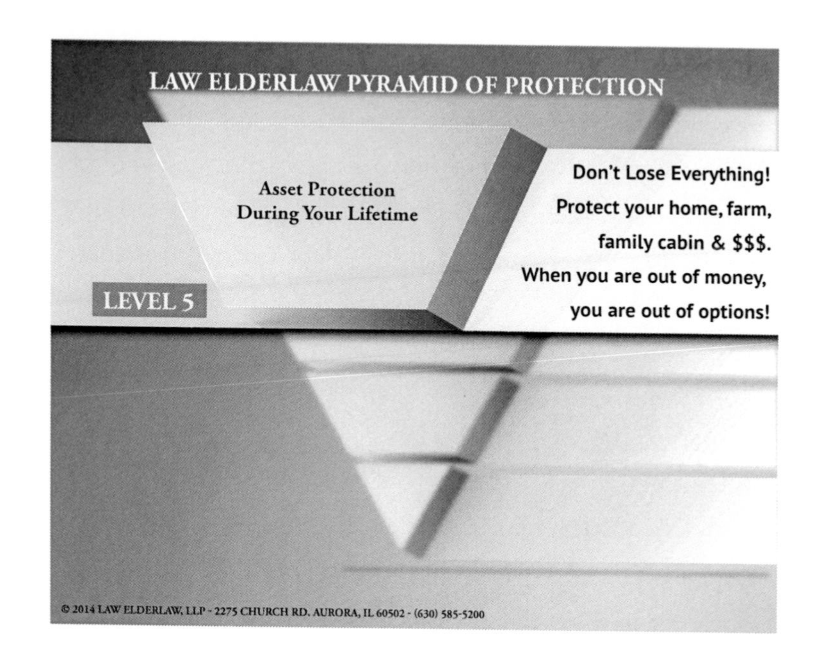

LEVEL 5: ASSET PROTECTION DURING YOUR LIFETIME

When we started Law ElderLaw, we focused primarily on Medicaid crisis asset protection. Asset protection during your lifetime is complex and adversarial. You have to remember that if you're trying to keep assets protected, then you're trying to keep them protected from someone, some organization, or some governmental body that wants to get to it. You have enemies! Asset protection during your lifetime is substantially complex and sophisticated planning, which is why it is listed at level five. You need to have a trustworthy attorney with tremendous experience in this area if you're going to be successful in protecting your assets during your lifetime.

We use wealth protection trusts, which are a type of flexible, irrevocable trusts. Our trust must survive the scrutiny of government bureaucrats and courtroom judges. These trusts are designed to keep you from losing everything when you get an unwelcome diagnosis such as Alzheimer's or Parkinson's disease. We have used these trusts to protect homes, farms, family cabins, and substantial sums of money. We use these trusts because our clients want to know that, if they are threatened with the loss of everything, they have done something to protect some portion of their estate from being completely destroyed. Our clients know that when you're out of money, you're out of options, and no one wants that to happen while they're still alive.

LEVEL 6: BUSINESS PLANNING—SUCCESSION, BUY-SELL AGREEMENTS, ASSET PROTECTION, AND TAX REDUCTION

In our typical workshops, we do not go through the ins and outs of business planning. Business planning is always customized to the facts and circumstances of the owners, their families, and their business. Tax attorney Zach Hesselbaum will explore different types of business-related asset protection in chapter 7.

Chapter 7

ASSET PROTECTION TOOLS FOR BUSINESS (PYRAMID OF PROTECTION LEVEL 6)

DON'T LOSE THE FAMILY FARM!

Will you be able to pass your business—and its income—along to your loved ones, or will it be lost to estate taxes, poor management, or predators and creditors? It's a question that gnaws at so many families before they come to see us at Law ElderLaw. The proverbial "family farm" might be an actual farm, or it might be a family-run business that you'd like to see carry on your legacy.

We can't tell you how often a client comes to us and says, "My brother tells me I need an LLC," or, "My financial advisor insists that I get an FLP." Well-meaning family members and others you trust may suggest ways for you to protect your business, but our role is to help you make a wise decision about the most appropriate asset protection and/or business entity for *you*. In this chapter, we'll look at several different strategies for protecting your business. Ultimately, you will probably need to seek guidance from a competent advisor who will help you achieve your goals by evaluating your needs based on all the factors in your situation.

FAMILY LIMITED PARTNERSHIPS (FLP)

It seems like just about every TV personality wants to sell you a Family Limited Partnership (FLP). They're all over the television, the radio, and even YouTube. In some situations, an FLP can indeed be a wonderful tool for families who do business together, whether they own rental property, a small business, a valuable collection, or a family farm. In our office, we most often see families who own and operate farm properties.

The most common use of an FLP is to provide a vehicle for the high-net-worth business owner to spread their wealth to family members both inside and outside the business. It can be helpful for estate tax avoidance after the death of the matriarch and/or patriarch founders of the business. Using an FLP can help lower or, in some instances, even eliminate estate taxes—not to mention helping your family avoid probate. What's more, it can help lower income tax. This can be a valuable tool while you're still an active part of the family business.

The primary value of an FLP is to help guide a business transition from one generation to another both during life and after death. Let's look at the example of Robert and Eileen, who recently came into our office.

Robert and Eileen own a family farm. Their son, Jack, works on the farm with Robert. Jack is young and eager, but he's just learning the ropes of running a successful farm. Robert and Eileen want to maintain control over how the farm is run, but they also want to begin the transition of allowing Jack to take some responsibility for the farm.

Jack will eventually take over the farm entirely, but Robert and Eileen can start moving assets to him piece by piece, allowing them to retain control as Jack learns. With an FLP, they can simply change the partnership structure when they're ready to relinquish control entirely, but in the meantime they will continue to reap income and estate tax benefits.

How this works is that Robert and Eileen, as the primary owners, are the general partners—they manage and retain control over the partnership. They also control how income is distributed annually and retain the ability to transfer partnership principal assets to other family members. Jack becomes a limited partner, and he owns a percentage of partnership assets without control. They've begun by transferring $6 million in farm property to the FLP, as well as $1 million in farm equipment. Once funded, they distribute partnership shares based on percentage, naming themselves general partners and Jack as limited partner. They can continue to structure the gifting of partnership shares as time goes on. This saves the farm from being lost to the kinds of mistakes an inexperienced, young farmer might make, including the risk of loss due to creditors or the divorce of their son, Jack.

It also limits the liability of losing assets that now belong in the FLP. The law sees those assets as belonging to the partnership, and no longer belonging to Robert and Eileen. That means these assets are walled off from third-party creditors or predators—whether they're after Robert and Eileen, or Jack.

Once Jack is ready to have control over the family farm, Robert and Eileen can easily make that happen. It's as simple as changing the name of the general partner to Jack.

Fortunately, the FLP can be beneficial to more than just farming families. It can be a great solution for family businesses being passed down to younger generations, families that own rental properties, or even folks with substantial collections (such as sports memorabilia, rare coins, or stamps).

One of the downsides of an FLP is that it's fairly complicated to administer successfully. Because family members become partners in a membership, the FLP becomes its own registered entity. This means it also has annual tax filings separate from any of the family members. The entity also has to be registered with the state of incorporation, which requires annual filings and fees.

If you've ever bought something off an infomercial, you know the feeling of great excitement—excitement that the chopper/slicer/french-fry-maker is going to solve all your problems, but it never works the way they showed you on the commercial. You can be sure that estate planning tools sold through the TV or the internet work much the same way. The promotional hype oversimplifies the realities, and in the end the over-hyped concept may not give you the results you were looking for. Nonetheless, with a trustworthy, experienced team of advisors, this concept can yield enormous benefits to the right family and the right family business.

By the same token, when you're looking for a piece of equipment to do the job and you want the right tool, you'll likely go to the appropriate store and ask a salesperson. They can help you choose the tool you need for your situation—for example, if you have a small yard, you probably don't want a riding lawn mower. Family limited partnerships may be something a financial planner, accountant, or friend has told you will help—even if, in reality, they're not the best tool for the goals you want to accomplish.

For example, Bill and Barbra came into our office, sure that an FLP was the right product for them. Their financial planner wanted to sell it to them, and had told them it was a good legal strategy. Bill and Barbra had a retirement account of about $350,000 and a savings account of $197,000. They also had a modest home and a few other assets.

As we worked with them and their financial planner, it became clear that an FLP wasn't appropriate for their particular situation. It simply wouldn't give them the most benefit for their asset structure. Their financial planner still insisted that it was the way to go. We sat down with the financial planner and told him that we wanted to make sure Bill and Barbra had a fully integrated legal and financial plan. We looked at what their goals were: they wanted asset protection, which is more simply provided through other estate planning tools. They needed the type of plan that we put together for honest, hardworking families who've saved their pennies and want to have enough money to get comfortably through the rest of their lives.

Tax benefits are important, but plans must be viewed holistically, keeping in mind possible tax-related and family challenges in the next five years and beyond. This is vital because if there is even a minor chance long-term care could be needed, failing to plan ahead could result in disaster. Since 70% of us will spend some time in a nursing home during our lifetimes, it's something we *all* need to plan for. Questions that Bill and Barbra should be asking are:

- Will Bill need nursing home care down the line, since he has diabetes and some other chronic issues that could worsen over time?

- Will Barbra have enough to live off after all of Bill's care costs are paid?

- What benefits are available to help pay for care as Bill and Barbra age? Will their financial products allow them to qualify for those benefits?

A typical FLP doesn't have protection against Medicaid, and their savings would be considered an available asset, meaning they couldn't qualify for benefits. Once Bill and Barbra's financial advisor had a better understanding of why this particular tool wasn't appropriate for them, he agreed—it wasn't a good fit. With that in mind, we went another route to help them achieve their goals.

LIMITED LIABILITY COMPANY (LLC)

A Limited Liability Company (LLC) is one of the most prominently used tools for estate and asset protection planning for businesses or individuals. We've seen TV commercials with cheerleaders advertising them, but, as we discussed before, just because it's on TV doesn't mean it's the right tool for your unique goals. On the other hand, it very well may be!

There are definitely some benefits to an LLC if you find that it fits your situation. For example, an LLC qualifies for the limited personal liability that corporations receive, while giving beneficial tax efficiency for partners/members. Income flows directly from the LLC side to the members, while avoiding corporate tax rates, yet maintaining limited personal liability for the members.

In addition, members of an LLC do not put their personal assets at risk as they enter into business opportunities. There are, of course, exceptions to this rule, but generally, LLCs put at risk only assets actually funded into and owned by the LLC. LLCs can be excellent tools for small business owners because they offer personal protections in case they're sued by a disgruntled customer or creditor.

Let's look at our client George for an example of a well-managed LLC that protects personal assets. George was a successful investment banker for many years, and has assets worth about $5 million. He retired from his previous career and started a new business that he enjoys with his daughter Melissa. Together they own a shop that sells Christmas ornaments and decorations year round. They run a successful and honest business.

Last year a restaurant owner ordered roughly $150,000 of Christmas lights. George and Melissa fulfilled the order, but when it arrived at the restaurant, the owner disliked the color of the lights, considered them defective, and threatened to sue George and Melissa's business for the full amount.

Without an LLC, the business owner could have come after George's personal wealth of $5 million. However, since the liability is limited by the LLC, only the assets of the LLC could be taken. At the time, the LLC had an inventory valued at $75,000 and $5,000 in receivables. This money was in danger, but not George's home or other assets. With an LLC properly in place and administratively maintained, George and Melissa avoided the worst-case scenario.

You should note that LLCs can be defective if the partners created the LLC incorrectly, or if it was rendered inadequate because they did not keep the annual required minutes of meetings, they forgot to update paperwork, and similar issues. There's a lot to remember! That's another benefit of working with a qualified attorney:

someone is by your side to help ensure things are created and managed appropriately.

One of the most common things we hear about LLCs is, “Well, an attorney drafted this for me some time ago, and I’m not really sure what I have.” Our team often has to clear these sorts of situations up. Maybe the client just needs to have things explained to them, or often, we find there are defects. For example, it might have been a perfectly fine LLC when it was drafted, but it was never funded, so it is useless. Funding is the process by which ownership of assets is transferred to your specific estate planning/business planning entity, whether it is an FLP, LLC, or trust. These are living breathing documents that are very powerful, but they will not work until they actually own assets (or until we put things in the “box,” to reference our earlier analogy). Therefore, a detailed retitling process must be undertaken to change ownership of assets.

Clients are often surprised at how difficult the funding process can be. For example, it is not uncommon for a person operating rental properties to have a well-drafted LLC, but they have failed to transfer ownership of the rental properties via deed into the name of the LLC. Therefore, after years of thinking they had a perfectly drafted LLC, they realize that, if something would have happened to the assets the LLC was designed to protect, they were actually left naked and exposed. Funding is a critical part of the entire estate planning process, and finding legal and financial advisors that put funding at a premium is imperative to having your plan function as designed.

Zach on Funding . . .

Not all assets can be simply moved around and retitled. When simply transferred, some assets can have unforeseen penalties and tax issues. Some of these are:

- **Annuities** are contracts that create specific sets of rules, and transferring ownership of these contracts often can give rise to early withdrawal penalties or unforeseen taxation on deferred income. Detailed analysis should be completed before transferring annuities as part of the funding process.

- **Homestead real estate** requires particularly sensitive planning. Keeping in mind real estate tax benefits, such as the homestead exemption and senior freeze, is important; improper transfer of residences can result in the loss of these beneficial exemptions. Further, maintaining a residence of homestead provides substantial exemptions of capital gains on sale—benefits that can be lost with improper transfers of homestead real estate. Finally, if transferring a residence to a non-spousal third party, a tax basis analysis should be completed to inform all parties of potential capital gain taxation upon the sale of the residence.

- **Qualified funds (IRAs, 401(k)s, 403(b)s, SEP)** must be reviewed for tax issues that will arise when transferred into a trust. If you don't review funding consequences beforehand, there could be big trouble ahead! Generally, qualified funds cannot be owned by a trust during the owner's lifetime. In specific cases, trusts can serve as beneficiaries. However, careful analysis and drafting should be completed to make sure the trusts serving as beneficiaries are "qualified trusts" to handle these specific types of funds. Failure to property analyze qualified funds could result in 100% income taxation on these accounts either during the owner's lifetime or upon transfer to the beneficiary. This could have devastating effects, such as increasing a retiree's Medicare premiums or requirement of quarterly tax payments.

IRREVOCABLE LIFE INSURANCE TRUST (ILIT)

An Irrevocable Life Insurance Trust, or ILIT, is an excellent and powerful estate planning document that, if used properly, can provide amazing results. It's also one of the trickiest tools to use because it has to be managed just right in order to work.

An ILIT is another tool used for individuals or couples with a high net worth—currently more than about $5 million per person, or about $10 million for the couple. Couples with less than $10 million in assets are better served by a traditional, foundational, trust-based estate plan.

ILITs are best used for someone who is more than likely to pass away with a taxable estate. Essentially, it removes from the estate tax calculation funds that would be taxable, by investing in a life insurance policy owned by the ILIT that falls outside a taxpayer's estate when managed appropriately by the trustee. This is a powerful way to make sure liquid assets are available for families to pay estate tax bills after a high-net-worth individual's death, or to simply insure the funding of a particular legacy interest.

Let's take a look at our client Dan. He owns a substantial farm here in Illinois that's been passed down in his family for over 100 years, and he intends to help it stay with his family for many years to come. While Dan has lived frugally and simply all his life, his land is worth $10–$15 million—he's technically a multi-millionaire and will be taxed as such when he passes away. The problem is that those millions are tied up in the actual ground where the farm sits; Dan's liquid assets are modest and certainly not enough to pay a looming estate tax bill. Dan's kids have good jobs—his oldest son works with him on the farm, and his daughter runs a shop in town. But, while they're hardworking and able to support themselves, Dan knows that as beneficiaries, they won't have the cash to pay the estate taxes on the family farm they'll inherit. Sadly, in most cases when the patriarch of a large farm passes away, the beneficiaries are forced to sell large chunks of their family land to pay for the estate taxes.

Fortunately for Dan's family, since he's planned ahead and created an ILIT, in conjunction with a comprehensive estate plan, his kids will have the money they need to pay the estate taxes due upon Dan's death. In this situation the ILIT, an irrevocable trust with a third party or professional trustee, is established to fund tax needs upon Dan's death. This trust is funded with a life insurance policy with annual premiums paid in a very specific manner during Dan's life. The proceeds of the life insurance policy at Dan's death pass tax-free to the beneficiaries and remain outside of Dan's estate tax calculation if the trust is managed appropriately during Dan's life.

The life insurance provides Dan's kids with enough liquid funds so they can pay the tax bill on the land they'll inherit without having to sell off any of the sacred property. Dan's looking out for his kids and striving to help them save the family farm.

This special trust is created a number of years before the trustmaker's death and is funded by annual gifts from the trustmaker. The trustee then pays a premium on a life insurance policy owned by the trust. Each year, very specific written notices need to be given to the beneficiaries of the trust. The purpose of the notices is to let the beneficiaries know they have a period of time in which they can access the money gifted into the trust each year. The intent of the gifts is to pay the premiums of the life insurance policy, not to enrich the beneficiaries, but the present interest created for the beneficiaries must be broadcast and provide a right of withdrawal. (The type of notice required is called a "Crummey notice.")

The hope is that the trust has educated beneficiaries who follow through and decide *not* to receive their current interest, but to wait for the final distribution. If a beneficiary decides that they want their interest in a particular year and take too much out, there may not be enough left for the premium. If there are not enough funds to pay the premiums, the life insurance policy may lapse and the funding of this plan falls apart. This could result in devastating estate tax bills that come due without funds available to pay.

An ILIT is difficult to administer—it's a lot to manage. You need an experienced legal advisor to handle the administration of an ILIT because there's a high probability of error, which will cause the trust to fail.

The ILIT is not a Swiss army knife that everyone should be using. It's usually best in a high-net-worth situation where you're trying to accomplish specific, unique estate planning goals. Those goals could range from funding a specific charitable interest upon death; funding the operations of a business post-death; or funding a legacy, including scholarship funds or foundations, after the estate tax bills have been paid.

DOMESTIC ASSET PROTECTION

Another little-known secret to asset-protection is that when you create a trust or register your business, it doesn't have to be under the jurisdiction of the same state in which you (or the business) reside. Asset protection laws in some states offer far more protection than in Illinois. We often recommend to our clients that they purposefully register their business or trust in a state that is more protective of the person creating it.

This can be critically important for lots of reasons, but especially helpful to both reduce taxes and protect against additional liability. It can be used to protect against those future unknowns that you or your business might otherwise be liable for, including:

- Accidents not fully covered by insurance
- Slip and falls
- Personal or business debt
- Issues with renters at rental properties
- Failed business deals

The way this works is that you set up specific assets to protect yourself from those unknowable liabilities, and you place the trust or business in any state you'd like—a state you feel has laws that provide you, as the trust creator or business owner, with the best protections.

The list of which states are best for asset protection changes each year. Our office monitors rankings that are published on an annual basis, listing which states are best for asset protection. This allows you to put law on your side for your benefit—even if you and your attorney are located in Illinois.

DON'T LOSE THE FAMILY FARM—NOW OR AFTER YOU'RE GONE

With these tools in mind, you may find you've got a better idea of how to plan for your business. If there's anything we want you to remember, it's that working with a qualified elder law estate planning attorney with business-specific experience is vital to ensure everything runs smoothly. Sure, it's possible to use an attorney who knows only the operational aspects of the business, but that attorney may not be considering other factors that could negatively impact the business, such as creditors, predators, tax ambiguities, and long-term care costs of its aging owners.

Be wary of do-it-yourself asset protection, which makes you the "lawyer." Documents downloaded from the internet can be, at the very least, missing important protections and, at their worst, completely disastrous for your family. It is your responsibility to understand the weaknesses, vulnerabilities, and administration burdens associated with making your plan work. In addition, remember that you have "enemies." When your plan is attacked by a creditor, they will be represented by a debt collection attorney with the training and resources to attack the shield you constructed. Be smart! Use an experienced, focused law firm to stand with you and to protect you with the best asset protection shield in their arsenal. If you do this on your own or with a general practitioner, be sure you know what you're getting into, with the whole plan in mind, before you create any documents.

There are so many great options for business owners—and these are just a few of the scenarios we see in our firm on a regular basis. The key is to have a holistic approach to the process and to start planning now. The sooner you plan, the more options available to you. These and other tools can help you while you're alive, well, and running your business, and when you've passed it to the next generation.

Chapter 8

SOCIAL SECURITY AND RETIREMENT INCOME

WHAT WOMEN REALLY NEED TO KNOW ABOUT THEIR FUTURE FUNDS

Social Security is our government's income solution for the aging American. The *idea* behind Social Security was fabulous: provide money on a monthly basis to help our senior community during their golden years. The reality is that with costs on the rise, Social Security goes only so far financially, and standalone Social Security is not enough these days. Living off a dual Social Security income in a married situation isn't easy without other income, such as a company pension or interest and dividends from savings and/or investments.

Things can, and often do, get much worse after the death of one spouse. When you lose your beloved spouse, the government's rules place you into what we call the "Social Security shuffle." This isn't a fancy new dance step, but the beginning of the loss of income. Uncle Sam sends you a letter explaining they will now discontinue one of the two Social Security checks; you do get to keep the larger one.

Here is an example: Beth and Roger are a married couple. Roger gets $1,300 of Social Security income and Beth gets $525. If Roger dies before Beth, Beth "inherits" Roger's Social Security check of $1,300. However, she does *not* retain her own Social Security check of $525. She gets the larger of the two; therefore, the household income drops at Roger's death by her Social Security amount ($525 per month).

But it gets worse. Let's also assume that Roger had a pension from his industrial job. His defined benefit pension was $1,100 per month. We are frequently surprised at how few people can accurately describe what happens to their pension income when they die! Typically, one of these scenarios applies:

- **Straight life pension:** The pension dies when the participant dies. So in this scenario Beth will get **$0.00 per month**.

- **75 percent, 50 percent, 25 percent, or some other percentage of the pension income:**

The surviving spouse is named as a percentage beneficiary, *but* the monthly pension benefit is a percentage of the original pension, even while Roger is alive. So, for Roger, a 50-percent pension for his wife may have resulted in his pension check being reduced from $1,100 to perhaps $980 while he was alive to collect it—and a 50-percent survivor pension benefit for Beth would mean her new pension income would be 50 percent of Roger's $980, or **$490 per month**.

- **Survivor:** Here the spouse would get 100 percent of the spouse's pension amount. With this option Roger's pension would have been significantly reduced from the straight life pension amount of $1,100. An educated guess might be **$780 per month**.

Again, we can only guesstimate these figures, because each defined benefit plan is built differently, and the plan's actuarial assumptions define these figures. So the numbers above are just to give you an idea of what different pension amounts for Roger might look like.

Let's look at the household income if Roger dies and Beth had a 50-percent survivor pension:

Roger still living: $980 pension

+ $1,300 Roger's Social Security

+ $525 Beth's Social Security

= $2,805 of household income per month

Roger deceased: $490 50-percent survivor pension

+ $1,300 "inherited" Social Security

= $1,790 of household income per month

Result: The overall household income is reduced by over 36 percent! That is a significant monetary loss.

It's also necessary to consider the impact of what health insurance will cost Beth, especially if Roger's retirement plan does not provide a widow's healthcare coverage plan. The results could be financially devastating.

A Personal Insight from Rick . . .

When one of my loved ones died, I was surprised to learn of some of the decisions he had made regarding his retirement planning. He left his wife in a difficult spot. You see, the day before he died, they had a family income that included his pension of roughly $1,200 a month, his Social Security check of $1,200 a month, and her Social Security check of approximately $400 a month. So their total monthly income was $2,800. Unfortunately, the day after he died, his wife's income plummeted from $2,800 per month to $1,200 per month.

That happened because at retirement he had decided to take a straight life pension from his employer. A straight life pension provides you what I call the "daddy-size" check. He could have chosen to take the "daddy-and-mommy size" check, but that check would have been smaller. It would have, however, maximized the income for the survivor spouse, which would have been a much more loving and caring decision for the benefit of his wife.

He was a bright and capable man, so I really have no idea what he and his wife were thinking when they decided to take the larger check. Perhaps they mistakenly believed that they had sufficient assets to buffer the drop in income that she would have when he died. Perhaps they were in denial about death and disability. All I know is that by the time he passed away, his illness had cost them both a lot of money.

The situation Rick's parents faced is surprisingly common. Many times we ask our clients to recall whether they signed up for a straight life pension or a pension that had survivor benefits. At least 60 to 70 percent of the time our clients don't remember, so we ask them to call the Human Resource Department at their old employer to find out. We really need to know what income is available to the survivor spouse when we're doing retirement planning.

If you don't recall or you haven't made that decision yet, this chapter will be a benefit to you, especially if you're in the age range of 55 to 64. The goal of this chapter is to show that you do have control over making certain decisions on how you take your Social

Security benefits, and your decisions could mean anywhere from $30,000 to $300,000 of income over you and your spouse's life expectancy.

We must apologize to those who are uncomfortable with us talking about the male as the person that has the higher pension and/or higher Social Security and the wife having a lower pension and a lower Social Security. That is the circumstance we currently deal with 95 percent of the time. In the next generation of couples coming up, we know the woman often has a higher income than her spouse. That was a very rare situation for the boomers—the World War II generation, the Korean War generation, and the Vietnam War generation. I (Rick) am a boomer myself, and in this chapter I will share my experiences in serving the three generations that I have just noted.

SOCIAL SECURITY THEN AND NOW

In the 1930s, the country began to think about planning to provide for the nation's elderly. A census reported that 6,634,000 people were over the age of 65, and this was 5.4 percent of the population. California and Wyoming enacted "old age pension" laws. On July 21, 1930, the Veteran's Administration was established. On June 27, 1934, the Railroad Retirement Act was approved by President Roosevelt but later declared unconstitutional. However, by the end August 1935, both the Railroad Retirement Act and the Social Security Act had become law.

At first, most people died before ever qualifying for Social Security or Medicare. In the 1960s and even 70s, the medical community was just beginning to extend human life. The first human heart transplant in the United States was performed in December 1967. Diagnosing cancer required exploratory surgery up until the 1970s. The real problem for these now programs seems to be that people are living longer—and the largest group of retirees, the baby boomers, are just starting to turn 65.

These days when we're working with pre-retirees and retirees, their big questions are how they should be taking Social Security and which assets they should be drawing from for retirement income. There's a lot of confusion about using Social Security money versus IRA money or money from brokerage accounts or other resources. This is something very important to know: taking retirement income from Social Security, retirement-qualified funds, and other assets is far more complicated than it was to acquire those assets in the first place. Nowadays many young people are choosing to do their investing using robots for that guidance. It's a lot easier to program a robot to analyze how you accumulate assets, but you need an extremely competent, experienced guide when it comes to calculating how you're going to be withdrawing assets over two lifetimes.

When you do this type of a calculation, you're juggling timing, budget, healthcare costs, and other resources that you may have available to you. A person needs to be very realistic about what their income will be and what their spending needs will be. We have seen many senior couples who over-consume in the early part of their retirement years with the expectation that they are going to die relatively soon after retirement. Many of them have been shocked to realize that their life expectancy is far longer than what their parents' life expectancy was. These days if you reached the age of 65, life expectancy is now 84 years for men and 87 years for women. Of women who are age 65, 25 percent will reach age 90, and 10 percent will reach age 100.

Many people have analyzed how important Social Security is to seniors. For the average United States senior citizen, Social Security provides about 40 percent of what the retiree's income was prior to retirement. Obviously there are many seniors whose sole source of income is Social Security, so it is providing 100 percent of their current income. But it may well represent only 40 percent of the income they had prior to retirement. Quality Social Security planning focuses on providing seniors with income that will last for the lifetimes of both the husband and the wife. A high-income retiree can expect that their Social Security will represent only 20 percent of their pre-retirement income. So, it can often be very difficult for high-income retirees to adjust their lifestyles to a lower retirement income of Social Security plus a reasonable, sustainable withdrawal rate from their assets.

These calculations and realities have been greatly and negatively impacted by the low-interest-rate environment that has been forced upon us by the Federal Reserve and economic conditions. When we work with our clients and their advisors, our goal is basically to help them go through the balancing act of looking at Social Security, pensions, and withdrawals from their other resources. One of the things we ask ourselves is this: if a client retires at 62, should he file for Social Security at 62? Should the client take small withdrawals from the IRA or other resources? Or, based on our calculations, is a better decision to delay the claiming of all Social Security benefits to some future time, even possibly up to the age of 70?

It may not surprise you that the majority of individuals really want to start taking their Social Security as quickly as possible. It doesn't make any sense to them to think about draining down other assets any faster than necessary. They see Social Security as a faucet, and they'd like to turn on that stream of income as quickly as possible. Here in our law firm we are an unusual breed. We are lawyers who do math. We use sophisticated computer programs to calculate expected benefits from various sources such as Social Security, IRAs, and other assets. What we have learned is this: delaying Social Security benefits can result in a much higher future benefit and value, even if it turns out that the client initially has to withdraw monies from their IRA or other assets quickly.

DOING THE MATH

We often run a calculation to determine what the breakeven point is in the event that a client chooses to delay benefits. It's important to think here about both the husband and wife's life expectancy. As we stated earlier in this chapter, the woman's life expectancy is longer than her husband's. And many of us know women who live 15 years or more after their husbands have passed away. To calculate the total value of a stream of income from Social Security, you look at the longevity of the individual who will live the longest. If you really want to get the most out of Social Security, you want to provide the greatest benefit over time so that the survivor spouse is not impoverished at the time of the first death.

Here's a summary of a few of those surprises that we learn as we do this type of retirement planning calculations. Basically we're, again, looking at a budget and a withdrawal rate and the sources of income and the assets.

We do a retirement spending calculation. We also add to that a calculation based on the value expectation of increase in earnings on the assets. And we have to calculate the cost of taxes from the withdrawal from various assets. We also throw into the mix a variety of scenarios based on timing of claiming Social Security benefits. In addition to just claiming Social Security benefits, we also look at what is the best way to use the Social Security spousal benefit compared to an individual's actual benefit. That plays into the situation where one of the spouses has a significantly lower Social Security based on their own earnings.

The calculations are not something that the typical client would do for themselves, and the results are often shocking to our clients. Most clients just assume that they should retire at 62 with what they think is a great Social Security check and perhaps even a large IRA and pension and other assets. What they fail to take into their calculation is how destructive future inflation will be on their income. If you think about even a 3-percent inflation factor, then if you expected to spend $80,000 a year in 2015, you would need $107,513 to equal the same dollar value ten years from now. Twenty years from now you would need $144,489 per year to have the same buying power. And amazingly, thirty years from now you would need $194,181. As you think about those numbers, from 62 years of age to 92 years of age is 30 years. So for the husband and wife who expect to spend

$80,000 a year in 2015, for that survivor spouse to have that equivalent income when she or he is 92, they'll need to have $194,181 per year.

Many of our clients are actually angry when they think about how high their taxes are going to be in retirement. They were told over the years that if they saved their money in their IRA, when they are old and want to use it they will be in a lower tax bracket. Well, taxes are quite expensive and they just don't go away. Many times we work with our clients to calculate what the cost factor is on their retirement withdrawal rate. They need to know whether they're going to be paying 15 percent, 18 percent, or more in taxes. In addition, it is also shocking and alarming to clients when they think about how quickly their retirement assets will dissipate once they start to withdraw from them. And of course no one wants to be hit by the double whammy of not only withdrawing assets, but going through a period like 2008–2009 where the actual value of their assets declines by 50 percent on top of their withdrawal of substantial funds every year.

We have worked with a number of clients who have been devastated by the combination of poor investment return and withdrawal of their income. That's the sort of scenario that winds up making a senior couple a burden on their children, or as women are often concerned about, becoming a "bag lady."

A key message that we want to get through to you is this: when you're dealing with retirement income withdrawal planning, you are constantly looking at a lot of variables. We've got the balance, the timing of claiming for Social Security, the budget you expect to live on, and all of your possible sources of income. If you are like the majority and you insist on retiring early and filing for Social Security, you will probably have to lower your budget. Many times we can show our clients how they can have a much more comfortable retirement if they're willing to work longer, save more money, and rethink how to utilize their assets. We will do the math analysis to give you ideas to work with.

We've given you an overview of Social Security. It gets a lot more complicated! If you're looking for more information than what we've provided above, keep reading, and we'll go into more detail on some important topics. Otherwise, go ahead to the next chapter.

SPECIFICS ON THE SOCIAL SECURITY BASICS

Now we'll discuss more specifically about how Social Security works and some strategies to get the most out of it for the sake of the longest-living spouse. We can't explain much more about Social Security without first introducing a number of terms and definitions, so brace yourself for a mouthful of acronyms.

The **Primary Insurance Amount (PIA)** is the base benefit amount which a retiree is entitled to receive, calculated from their Social Security contributions during their career. All adjustments to Social Security benefits are determined based from the PIA, which is determined by taking an indexed average of the highest 35 years of taxable contributions. That determination is referred to as the **Average Indexed Monthly Earnings (AIME)**. You are eligible for PIA, as determined by AIME, at the **Full Retirement Age (FRA)**, which is the age at which Social Security deems that you as the claimant should receive your full benefit. Currently the FRA ranges between 65 and 67 years of age, depending upon your date of birth.

The next term is the **Actuarial Reduction**, which is a permanent penalty imposed on the monthly benefit when Social Security is claimed before the FRA. **Delayed Retirement Credits (DRC)** is the permanent increase in benefits awarded to a Social Security claimant who chooses to claim after FRA. Here is a basic concept regarding either claiming early or claiming later than the FRA. When a person files for their benefit at the age of 62, their benefit is reduced according to the actuarial reductions. Actuaries are people who make calculations on the cost of a risk. The Social Security actuary is trying to calculate the Social Security claimant's life expectancy and earnings, and then make sure that the claimant receives the same amount of money over time, regardless of whether he or she claims early or late. So the actuaries have calculated what kind of reduction there would be for early claiming and what kind of benefit there would be for later claiming. What they do not take into account is very important to the surviving spouse: they do not calculate what the value of claiming late would be to the surviving spouse. This is the really big deal of this chapter! When the person with the higher Social Security benefit is the one to die first, then the income benefit to the surviving spouse is greatly increased when the Social Security benefit was delayed up to the age of 70.

If we assume that the Social Security claimant is a boomer, then that person was born in the timeframe in which the FRA is 66 years of age. If a boomer chooses to claim their full benefit at the age of 62, they will receive a 25-percent reduction from what they would receive at full retirement age. On the other hand, if that boomer chooses to delay claiming their full benefit until the age of 70, they will receive 32 percent more than the primary insurance amount that they would have received at FRA. In summary, if you claim at 62, your benefit is 25 percent less than it would have been at FRA. If you claim at 70, your benefit is 32 percent higher than at FRA. Without running complex calculations to determine possible outcomes for you and your spouse, you will never know what the best thing to do is. There are many capable financial advisors at our law firm who are trained to do that type of analysis on your behalf.

The next term, the **Cost of Living Adjustment (COLA)** is Social Security's inflation protection that increases the benefit amount every year. The effect of COLA is to increase the impact of both the actuary deductions for those who claim early or the delayed retirement credits for those who claim later. In other words, when you claim early, the COLA is factored off of a low amount. When you claim late, the COLA is factored off of a higher amount. The **excess earnings test** is the calculation that determines a penalty for money earned for those who claimed prior to full retirement age.

When a person claims Social Security benefits before FRA and they continue to earn income, there is a possibility of a penalty. That penalty is actually a reduction in the amount of money that will be withheld from your Social Security check, based on the amount of earnings you have. When you earn money in the years before the year in which you reach FRA, there will be a reduction of $2 of the excess earnings over $15,480: $1 of Social Security benefits are withheld for each $2 earned over that threshold. That threshold is modified on an annual basis.

In the year when the Social Security claimant reaches the FRA, there is a different factor used to determine withholding. In that year, for every $3 of excess earnings over $41,400, there will be $1 of Social Security benefits withheld; however, those withheld benefits are factored back in to your overall Social Security income over your lifetime after you reach the FRA.

RULES OF COUPLES PLANNING

In the world of Social Security, couples need to think about not only their own Social Security benefit, but also the Social Security benefit of their spouse while that spouse is alive, and the spousal benefit to the surviving spouse after a spouse has died. There are different categories of benefits. One is called a **spousal benefit** and the other is called the **survivor benefit**. The spousal benefit can be summarized as one-half of the spouse's PIA. The survivor benefit is different. When your spouse has died, if his/her Social Security check was higher than yours, then you may drop your Social Security benefit and stand into the shoes of your spouse. In that situation, the surviving spouse receives the decedent's entire benefit.

So, the highest possible spousal benefit is available to a couple when both claim at FRA (which could be anywhere between 65 and 67). The highest possible survivor benefit occurs when the person who has the highest Social Security benefit (usually the husband), claims for Social Security at the age of 70 and when the wife claims at her FRA. When it comes to spousal benefits, if a spouse applies for a spousal benefit, there will be a 35-percent reduction from what the spousal benefit would be at the full retirement age. Please note that that is a bigger reduction than if you were applying for your own benefit based on your own earnings record. The survivor benefit is also subject to actuarial reductions and delayed retirement increases, as those are applied to the higher-earning spouse's Social Security checks. However, at the time of his or her death, the surviving spouse steps into the shoes of the deceased and receives 100 percent of those benefits.

THREE RULES FOR DETERMINING SPOUSAL BENEFITS

There are three special rules of determining spousal benefits. The first rule is spousal benefit entitlement restrictions in which you cannot claim a spousal benefit until your spouse claims his/her own Social Security benefit. Second, there is a way to have a spousal-only benefit created when the spouse with the higher earnings record files for Social Security but claims restrictions upon the scope of the benefit they are applying for. In other words, if the husband is the higher earner, and he reaches FRA and files for Social Security benefits but restricts the benefit they wish to receive to a spousal benefit, then the husband can delay the date in which they claim their own benefit based on their own earnings. Nonetheless, at full retirement age they will have triggered the payment of a spousal benefit based on their PIA at FRA. This is a great way to actually get the best of both worlds.

There is also a concept known as the **deemed filing rule**: when a spouse files before their FRA, they are deemed to have filed for all available benefits unless they specifically restrict their request. For example, if Henry files for Social Security at age 62, then he is deemed to have filed for both his own benefit and any available spousal benefit. Please note this has a huge impact on what can be received by both current and any past spouses.

FILING STRATEGIES

Here's a review of what we call the **File and Suspend Strategy**. When the spouse with the higher earning record files at FRA, they may restrict their filing to claiming the spousal benefit. At that particular moment, their spouse will receive one-half of the PIA of the filing spouse. The spouse who filed with restrictions may suspend the receipt of their own benefit until the age of 70. At age 70, the filing spouse now activates full benefits for themselves based on their earnings record plus the 32 percent. The higher benefit spouse continues to receive the maximum benefit, inflated by the COLA, until their death. At the time of their death, their surviving spouse claims the survivor benefit and now receives the maximum survivor benefit, which is 100 percent of the higher earning spouse's Social Security benefit. If a couple suspects that the wife will live longer than the husband, and the husband is the higher benefit spouse, then using the File and Suspend Strategy to benefit his wife is one of the most loving things a husband can do.

Another strategy is called the **Get Money Now and Get More Money Later Strategy** or the **Claim Now and Claim Later Strategy**. This concept differs from the File and Suspend in the following manner. In this situation, the spouse with the lower earnings goes ahead and files for early benefits at the age of 62. Of course, they will receive a reduced benefit from what they would have received at FRA, but nonetheless, they begin to receive a monthly check. At the time the early-filing spouse receives their reduced benefit, the spouse who has the higher earnings record actually claims a spousal-only benefit off of the lower-earning spouse's benefit and does not file for their own full benefit. This spousal-only benefit may be a small amount of potentially several hundred dollars, but that money can quickly add up over the years.

The spouse who files and claims the spousal-only benefit is at full retirement age. When the spouse at FRA files for the spousal benefit only, they delay and suspend their own benefit, trying to wait until age 70 to file. At the age of 70, the higher-earning spouse, who has been receiving the spousal-only benefit, now claims his own benefit. At that time, the lower-earning spouse drops her reduced benefit and applies for the spousal benefit off of the higher amount of the higher-earning spouse. That creates an increased check for the wife and a maximum benefit for the husband. The husband continues to receive the maximum benefit until his death. At his death, his wife claims a survivor benefit and she jumps up to receiving the maximum survivor benefit, also adjusted upward by cost of living increases. This is another wonderful way to maximize benefits for both the husband and wife.

GOVERNMENT PENSIONS

It's important to understand that there are reductions in Social Security benefits when a claimant or a claimant's spouse is receiving a government pension. We'll briefly explain two important concepts, the **Government Pension Offset (GPO)** and the **Windfall Elimination Provision (WEP)**. The GPO applies whenever a *claimant spouse* is receiving a government pension for which no Social Security was paid.

The penalty is an annual offset calculation where the spousal and survivor benefits are reduced by two thirds of whatever the governmental pension benefit is. In this particular situation we recommend that the claimant spouse delay claiming the Social Security benefit if it could allow for the receipt of a higher survivor benefit or allow for increased inflation protection.

The WEP is considered when the *claimant* is receiving a government pension and has had fewer than 30 years of Social Security contributing earnings. The WEP reduces the claimant's benefit when they are receiving other governmental pension benefits. It also impacts the spousal benefit, but it does not reduce the survivor benefit. Doing the calculations to determine the impact of the WEP is extremely complicated and must be undertaken by those who are well-versed in Social Security planning. The typical solution for people who are burdened by those penalties is this: if they want the Social Security benefit, they may need to work longer to reach beyond the 30 years of paying into Social Security. Of course, that is often not a realistic alternative.

A FEW FINAL CONSIDERATIONS

Our goal in calculating projected income and costs is to help married couples choose the claiming strategy that will maximize their income over the longevity of both of the partners. One also needs to do a break-even analysis if they choose to delay the receipt of Social Security monies. In addition, it's important to calculate how the couple will bridge the gap in income when they choose to delay Social Security. Bridging the gap in income is usually done by either having the higher-earning spouse work until age 70 or withdrawing funds from other assets that are earning a lower level of annual return than the increase in Social Security. It's important to keep in mind that the annual increase in Social Security income is guaranteed to be 8 percent per each year that you choose to delay between full retirement age and age 70. Outside of Social Security, there are very few sources of income with a governmental guarantee of an 8-percent yearly increase for four years—a 32-percent increase in income by delaying the higher spouse's claiming of full Social Security benefits. That is the big deal about Social Security planning.

Above we noted that there are certain penalties for taking early Social Security and continuing to work and earn money over certain thresholds. That's also part of what needs to be considered. Also, if your annual gross income as reported on your tax return is higher than $34,000 (single) or $44,000 (joint) you will be taxed on 85 percent of your Social Security benefits. That factor is not indexed for inflation. Therefore, every year more and more seniors are paying taxes on their Social Security, which means that some portion of their Social

Security increase is lost to the cost of taxation. Careful planning needs to be done to recognize the impact of higher earnings, not only on typical taxation but also on penalty Medicare taxes. For people who earn over $85,000 (single) or $320,000 (joint), there are substantial increased costs for Medicare Part B (medical insurance) coverage and the Medicare Part D (prescription drug) coverage. See www.medicare.gov for the costs that apply to your income range.

A final point to consider is long-term care planning. We have to recognize that the Social Security income that you have worked so hard to maximize will *not* be protected from being diverted to the cost of care in the event that the survivor needs long-term care and wishes to qualify for nursing home Medicaid. On the other hand, it is possible that lump sum distributions from pensions may potentially be protected through sophisticated nursing home Medicaid asset protection strategies. All of those concepts are constantly in a state of flux due to changing rules of the state and federal government. The best recommendation we can give you in that particular situation is to review your facts and circumstances with a capable elder law estate planner. See chapter 11 for more information on attributes to look for in an excellent elder law estate planner.

Chapter 9

AVOIDING THE COMMON POTHOLES

FROM UNEXPECTED CARE EXPENSES TO REMARRIAGE TO GIFTING

So far in this book, we've covered many important facets of the retirement ride, from Medicare to asset protection to Social Security. In this chapter we identify a number of potholes we often see our seniors encounter—some we've discussed already, some we haven't. They can make for a bumpy ride if you don't see them before you hit them and if you don't know how to avoid them.

MISUNDERSTANDING THE MARKET IN RELATION TO LONGEVITY

Most people do not understand the investments they have chosen. Since they don't understand the investments, it is not surprising that they do not have realistic expectations of the investments' performance.

One of Rick's favorite books about retirement planning is *High Expectations and False Dreams: One Hundred Years of Stock Market History Applied to Retirement Planning*, by Jim C. Otar. He notes that the average life cycle of an investor begins with accumulation of assets, followed by withdrawal.

In addition, the last 100 years have given each generation an opportunity to experience a long mega-bull market and a long mega-bear market, each lasting between 16 and 20 years. We are currently coming out of a mega-bear cycle, which can be predicted to extend to 2016 or even 2020, based on historical data. Retirees who begin withdrawals from their accumulated assets during a bear market are punished by both the depletion of their assets by withdrawal *and* by the decrease in the market value of their principal.

To avoid going broke in retirement, income investments must be maximized *and* total annual withdrawals from both stock and bond portfolios cannot exceed a paltry 4 percent per year. If withdrawal rates are held to 4 percent, then the accumulated principal stands a 90-percent chance of lasting through a 30-year retirement.

Unfortunately, most people choose to withdraw assets during their retirement based on two false assumptions:

- That future gains will make up for excessive withdrawals

- That their life expectancy will be similar to the lifespan of their parents

But medical advances have increased the life expectancy of U.S. citizens to 78.2 years. In 1950, the life expectancy of male children was 65 years, and a female child could expect to live to 71. In 2014, the average life expectancy of men who reach age 65 is 84.3; of women who reach 65, it's 86.6. Approximately 25 percent of women who reach age 65 will also reach age 90, and 10 percent will live to see 100.

You must take life expectancy risk into consideration along with very prudent asset withdrawal rates so that you do not find yourself out of money and out of options.

LONG-TERM CARE EXPENSES: UNEXPECTED ILLNESS SHOULD BE EXPECTED

We baby boomers saw our grandparents die of heart attacks, strokes, industrial accidents, agricultural accidents, and other "quick death" causes. When we were young, our peers died of unexpected illnesses and accidents. Now we're grandparents! As we look back over our post-WWII lifespans, medical advances have rescued us from many of the diseases and scourges of past ages. But now comes our time to go from healthy, vigorous seniors to seniors with memory and/or mobility issues. In a recent *AARP Magazine* article, it was reported that 70 percent of us will need long-term care! Ignore that statistic at the peril of you and your spouse.

As much as we all hate to admit it, there will likely come a time when we will need assistance in doing even some of the most basic daily living activities. In fact, in many cases, clients can more easily come to grips with concept of mortality, or death, than they can about their own morbidity, or the need for care—especially if that care involves long-term care or nursing homes.

It is at this stage where a picture must be painted in the client's mind as to what could happen—not just physically, but financially—if a need for care should arise. And the odds are very much in everyone's favor that, at some point in the future, the need for care *will* arise.

The phrase "long-term care" can mean many things, but the term can generally be defined as "the variety of services necessary for someone who requires some form of daily, ongoing assistance." Often, when a medical professional is qualifying an individual for a long-term care need, they will make a determination based on the person's ability—or inability—to perform various **activities of daily living (ADLs)**. The list of ADLs includes dressing, bathing, toileting, continence, transferring (from bed to chair), and eating (the ability to feed oneself).

Long-term care can be divided into various levels. These include:

- **Skilled care:** This type of care is considered to be medically necessary due to a physical or mental impairment. Skilled care constitutes around-the-clock care provided by licensed medical professionals under the direct supervision of a physician. Although many people tend to think of skilled care as the primary type of long-term care received, it really only accounts for less than 1 percent of all long-term care that is received.

- **Intermediate care:** This type of care is provided by a registered nurse (RN), licensed practical nurse (LPN), or a nurse's aide, under the supervision of a physician. Intermediate care is also considered to be medically necessary. It accounts for approximately 5 percent of all long-term care that is received.

- **Custodial care:** Custodial care is defined as receiving assistance with meeting ADL requirements. This refers to the receipt of supervisory or hands-on services provided to persons who suffer from a chronic illness that has been caused by a physical or cognitive impairment. This type of care is provided by a number of both professional (formal) and non-professional (informal) caregivers. It is not considered to be medically necessary, although the patient is not expected to recuperate from the physical or mental ailment that has caused them to need care. This type of care consists primarily of homemaker services such as cleaning the house, cooking, and other types of personal care assistance that helps the individual get through their daily routine. Custodial care accounts for nearly 95 percent of all long-term care that is received.

An individual may need long-term care for many different reasons. They could have a specific illness or injury that will require them to receive treatment and/or rehabilitation. They could have a cognitive or mental impairment such as Alzheimer's disease or impairments due to a stroke. Or, they could simply require assistance with basic daily activities.

Impairments that require the need for long-term care can be broken down into three types:

- **Acute impairments:** An acute impairment is a medical condition such as an accident-related injury, pneumonia, or a heart attack that strikes suddenly, but from which the individual may fully recover with the proper medical attention. Acute impairments do not in and of themselves cause a need for long-term care. For example, a stroke is considered to be an acute impairment that, if not caught in time, could cause death. If the individual survives, however, it may be with a chronic condition that actually creates the need for long-term care services.

- **Physical impairment:** A physical impairment is a treatable, but not typically curable, chronic condition. Common examples include emphysema, arthritis, diabetes, heart disease, and hypertension. Physical impairments that require long-term care are typically expressed in terms of difficulty performing ADLs.

- **Cognitive impairment:** Cognitive impairments are generally defined as a deterioration or loss of intellectual capacity as certified by a licensed healthcare practitioner, measured by clinical evidence and standardized tests, which can evaluate the individual's impairment in the areas of short- or long-term memory; orientation as to person, place, or time; deductive or abstract reasoning; and judgment as it relates to awareness of safety.

The individual who suffers from a cognitive impairment may be able to physically perform basic ADLs; however, they will likely need some type of supervision in doing so. Common causes of cognitive impairment include Alzheimer's disease, Parkinson's disease, and various other types of dementia. A cognitive impairment usually will lead to a permanent need for long-term care.

Although many people think only of skilled care when they hear the phrase "long-term care," it is important to remember that in reality, long-term care encompasses a wide array of medical, social, personal, supportive, and specialized housing services that are needed by individuals who have lost some capacity for self-care due to a chronic illness or a disabling condition.

It is also important to note that the goal of long-term care is not to *cure* an illness or condition, but rather to allow an individual the ability to attain and maintain an optimal level of day-to-day functioning. To avoid the pothole of being unprepared for a long-term illness, please take action to include some type of investment with long-term care coverage.

LONG-TERM CARE: A WOMAN'S NIGHTMARE

He looked into his wife's eyes and flatly stated, "I'll put a gun to my head before I ever go to a nursing home." Even if he really believes this, it is very seldom true. Men often voice macho denials of the realities of aging and long-term care. In truth, it is often his wife who bears the greater burden caused by his long-term care needs and her own aging challenges. Yes, his wife—like millions of her sisters—may spend years and all their money caring for her mate. She often selflessly provides in-home care until eventually the day comes when her strength is not enough to pick him up or keep him from wandering away from home. On that day, it might be a doctor, a discharge planner, or a policeman who finally speaks the real truth to her: "I'm sorry, ma'am. You cannot take care of him at home anymore." It is then that most women begin to experience phase two of the elder care nightmare. Most seniors do not realize that Medicare does not care about them when they need long-term care. Medicare was designed to take care of people who get well, but it doesn't provide much care for people who have chronic, long-term illness.

It has long been said that "women are the weaker sex"—but in the game of survival, men are the weaker sex and women are "fit for longevity." Women are more likely to live longer than men. Of individuals over age 90, women outnumber men nearly three-to-one; 90 percent of the people over age 100 are female. Among today's seniors, women are the primary caregivers in most families.

When we receive a call for assistance at our elder law office, most often the caller is a woman who is desperately seeking help with a spouse or a parent. Many times she is a daughter or daughter-in-law who has "drawn the short straw" in the family and must care for her father, mother, or in-law.

According to AARP, the typical caregiver in the United States is a 46-year-old woman. She has had some college education and she works outside the home at least part-time. Nonetheless, she still spends more than 20 hours a week providing care for her mother, father, or in-law. One in six caregivers in the United States provide 40 or more hours of care per week. Those same caregivers are often under high levels of physical and emotional stress due to the rigors of providing care for an older adult as well as providing for themselves and their own families. Many female caregivers make substantial sacrifices to accommodate the caregiving needs of aging seniors. These women must often cut short their professional work hours; they are often overlooked for promotions, they may lose employee benefits, they may need to take a leave of absence, some choose early retirement, and others are forced to end their careers entirely.

Women also dominate the ranks of professional healthcare workers. When one enters a long-term healthcare facility, it is immediately obvious that the staff is overwhelmingly female. Almost 90 percent of nurses, psychiatric workers, home care aides, and other members of the institutional and home healthcare field are women. Unfortunately, the majority of these workers are non-professional and are found at the low end of the pay scale with few employee benefits.

Women are at a greater risk than they realize of not having enough money after their husbands have died. The 2010 U.S. Census showed that the average annual income for women over 90 was $13,580, and the average annual income for men over 90 was $20,133. As discussed in the previous chapter, senior women receive far less Social Security income than men. Our Social Security system rewards those who work the longest and are paid the most. Women are penalized because they were often out of the workforce during the years they raised their children. Additionally, their jobs often paid less than the average for a male. Due to the loss of one Social Security check, the loss of some or all of her spouse's pension income, and the loss of savings that were spent on the husband's healthcare and final expenses, a woman often does not have enough money to maintain the standard of living that she enjoyed with her spouse.

Women face major challenges in living with independence and dignity as they age. The Kaiser Family Foundation estimates that 28 million of the current 42 million Medicare beneficiaries have at least two or more chronic conditions. Since men decline at a younger age than women, and Medicare pays little or nothing for healthcare costs related to the chronic care needs of a frail, older person, too often the burden of that care rests upon the women of the family. Lacking family help, most women face institutional placement in a nursing home, but millions of older women cannot afford long-term care services due to low income and lack of assets. Impoverished, they must rely upon Medicaid for their nursing home funding.

American seniors are provided with acute care (short-term care) coverage by the combination of Medicare, their own optional Medicare Supplement Insurance policy, and out-of-pocket payment of any deductible or healthcare expenses. Unfortunately for seniors, Medicare does *not* provide money for long-term care expenses, including diagnoses of Alzheimer's, Parkinson's, or other chronic diseases. (There are some important exceptions, such as kidney dialysis, ALS, and hospice.) Thus, our senior citizens "win the Medicare diagnosis lottery" when they receive a diagnosis of heart disease, diabetes, or another acute care problem. But every day, seniors lose this "diagnosis lottery" when they receive the bad news that they suffer from Alzheimer's or other dementias, arthritis, Parkinson's, stroke, or other chronic illnesses. When a husband must be relocated to a long-term care facility, the wife discovers that neither Medicare nor Medicare Supplement Insurance will pay the facility's $3,000 to $8,000 per month expense.

Quickly, she learns that Medicaid may not be available to provide nursing home costs in a Medicaid-certified nursing home bed, because she has "too much money." Her husband's care will be offset by Medicaid if—and only if—she and her husband meet stringent income and asset limitations. This is because Medicaid was originally designed to provide healthcare only for the poor.

There is no governmental benefit for long-term care that does not have a stringent income and asset limitation. If she and her husband have assets of more than roughly $101,000, then the state requires that they "spend down" their life savings, which Medicaid defines as "excess assets." When all excess assets have been spent on her husband's medical care, then the wife will find that Medicaid will also control *her* monthly income. Her income is restricted to $2,500 per month. If she has monthly income in excess of $2,500, then she must allocate the excess to her husband's cost of care.

Later, when her husband dies, she will receive even more bad news. As the "survivor spouse," she loses one of their two Social Security checks, and she often loses his pension. She has already spent assets to provide for her husband's care, so she is essentially in an impoverished state and may be forced to sell her home and spend the proceeds on her own long-term medical expenses. As a single person, she will not be provided with assistance by the state of Illinois or the federal government until she has become impoverished to the point of a paltry $2,000 or less in total assets. The indignity committed against her does not stop there, for now she must sign over all her income to the nursing home, except for a miserly "personal needs allowance" of only $30 per month. The loving wife who faithfully cared for her husband is now out of money and out of options. Thirty dollars per month will probably not be enough to provide her with the privilege of having her hair done. She is living the nightmare of long-term care in America.

Women need to be worried about their future life after their spouses have died. They need to take action and seek trustworthy advisors who can analyze what steps to take to protect themselves after their husbands are gone.

LEGAL POTHOLES FOR SENIORS GETTING MARRIED

In the Disney classic movie *Bambi,* when spring arrives, the adolescent Bambi notices that all of his male friends are becoming enchanted by young females of the same species. When Bambi asks the wise old owl what is wrong with them, he is gruffly told, "They are twitterpated!" As a law practice serving seniors and those who love them, we have observed that not just adolescents can become "twitterpated," but rather adults of all ages.

When seniors come to see us for premarital legal counseling, they are rarely interested in our left-brained, analytical advice regarding senior dating, partnership, and marriage. If you are reading this book, it's not likely that you are currently enslaved by such romantic enchantment, so here is some cautionary information that we give to our senior clients regarding marriage and/or remarriage.

It is important to understand that, as we age, it becomes highly likely that the health condition of the two partners will diverge. Young married couples moving through their twenties and onward towards their sixties can usually count on relatively good health. But as the famous actor Jimmy Stewart once said, "After 70, it's just patch-patch-patch." Seniors who are getting married need to understand that when they say "I do," they also are giving an implied and legally enforceable promise that says, "I will be obligated for your medical expenses."

It is very important to understand that neither medical providers nor the state of Illinois are barred by prenuptial agreements from collecting unpaid medical bills and/or reimbursement for Medicaid expenditures.

Zach on Second (or Even Third) Marriages . . .

Betty the Bimbo and Biff the Pool Boy

As Rick says, adults of all ages can become "twitterpated." Sometimes, adults who have been widowed can simply become lonely, which can result in poor choices for the sake of companionship. Don't get me wrong—not all second marriages are mistakes or have disastrous outcomes. However, you do have to consider the legal potholes of the second marriage and the blended family. Marriage is "for better or for worse and in sickness or in health," and this can create problems. It may be one thing for your dad to tap into the savings (or as you may think of it, "my inheritance") to care for your mom, but what about seeing it all spent on your stepmother, wicked or otherwise?

We have seen the lonely widower befriended by the bubbly, but broke, single gal who sees that her lifestyle could be greatly improved by marrying said lonely widower. We have seen the widow swept off her feet by the dashing but debt-laden Don Juan. The stories are too numerous to tell, but we often end up working with the children who are now watching their parent's life savings disappearing because of the second wife or husband and his or her deadbeat children. Both families are fighting for control over the healthcare issues of their respective biological parent and fighting to take control of the money before it is snatched up by the stepparent and his or her family. While everyone is healthy, they believe that they will keep assets separate and love will conquer all. When one of the spouses becomes incapacitated or dies, things can get very ugly, very fast.

Case in point: we were recently involved in a probate case where the surviving third wife and a child (stepchild to dad) of the second wife who is deceased are trying to raid the estate, which happens to be the family farm that was clearly intended to pass to the children of dad and mom (wife number one who passed away many years ago).

This is just food for thought for the love-starved widow or widower. You may be biting off more than you can chew and more than your family will be able to stomach in the long-run.

Rick on Powerless Powers of Attorney . . .

Almost every month I am invited to teach other lawyers at a continuing legal education forum. The typical invitation comes from either a county bar association or a national legal organization. My most requested class is entitled "Elder Law for Every Lawyer." In that class I share this concept about powerful powers of attorney for property between a husband and a wife. Please understand that most of the people who come to my office are couples who have had long marriages and usually are parents.

Most powers of attorney created by lawyers in our area use the Illinois statutory power of attorney for property as the foundational document. You can find this document by typing "Illinois statutory power of attorney property" into your internet search engine. The latest version became effective on January 1, 2015.

It has been my experience that most attorneys are familiar with the power of attorney for property form, but they are *not* familiar with the very special and important issues that confront a couple when one of the two of them receives a diagnosis of dementia, Alzheimer's, Parkinson's, ALS, MS, etc.

I was trained as a tax attorney. My job until the year 2000 had been focused on helping successful people arrange their personal and business matters to be tax-efficient. Estate plans for the well-to-do have three primary goals:

- Minimize or eliminate estate taxes
- Avoid the costs and delays of courtroom probate

- Provide for ease of post-death distribution of assets

As a tax attorney, I helped primarily with the first of those three goals, but that changed when, in the year 2000, I received a call from a family friend, Luise, that would change my professional life. She was panicked when she said, "Rick, Bob has been diagnosed with Alzheimer's. What are we going to do? Am I going to lose my home? Are we going to lose everything?"

I had never been asked these questions before, and my tax law training in high-net-worth estate planning was irrelevant. She needed solutions that would:

- Provide Alzheimer's care for her husband Bob,
- Protect the marital home for her, the healthy spouse, and
- Preserve sufficient resources to protect her lifestyle.

Unfortunately, Medicare provides only acute care reimbursement for citizens who are over 65, blind, or disabled. Medicare provides care only when you can get better. If your diagnosis requires long-term care, then Medicare does not care! Nursing home costs are usually paid for either from one's own savings or by the federal-state hybrid called Medicaid. Sadly, Medicaid benefits are based on a poverty concept. There are very strict limits regarding maximum dollar value of assets *and* monthly income. Thanks to Luise and Bob, I now concentrate my law practice on aging issues and long-term care.

This is what you need to know about powers of attorney for a 60-year-old or older adult. An attorney who focuses his/her practice in elder law *and* estate planning knows how to add nursing home Medicaid-specific powers to empower your trusted spouse/agent to be able to do the following things under the guidance of your legal counsel:

- Use gifting powers, consistent with your estate plan, to effectuate appropriate asset protection

- Take all reasonable and prudent actions allowable under Medicaid law to qualify the ill person for care, but also avoid doing anything that would make the ill person ineligible for benefits

- If appropriate, encourage an adult child to move into the home as a caretaker

- Allow a caretaker child to be paid a market rate for care

- Create and fund a special needs trust to provide you with dignity and supplemental monies, even though you may be receiving nursing home Medicaid

- And much more, subject to each client's circumstances and the law

If your power of attorney for property lacks these powers—which is the case 99.99 percent of the time—then you need to get a more powerful power of attorney!

FILL-IN-THE-BLANK ESTATE PLANS

Most estate planning has been reduced to a commodity service because the public thinks of their estate plan as just fill-in-the-blank documents. It's not your fault! Nevertheless, a fill-in-the-blank mindset leads to purchasing fill-in-the-blank online forms and/or hiring a really cheap fill-in-the-blank lawyer. This type of estate planning validates the timeworn saying, "You get what you pay for." If you purchase and fill in the blanks on your own estate documents, then *you* are the lawyer. If you choose a cheap fill-in-the-blank lawyer, you can expect that he/she intends to spend as little talent and time as possible to deliver to you a cookie-cutter estate plan.

Our clients choose our law firm because they have been told that we are "the best and most expensive" elder law estate planners. Almost all of our clients come to us by referral from other clients, other attorneys, or other professionals.

Our clients' estate plans affect their most important loved ones and the most valuable assets they own. They want someone to listen to their stories, fears, and hopes. They want their law firm to make the complicated seem simple and understandable. They want their advisors to think ahead and take appropriate steps to avoid future potholes.

One of the most time-consuming, tedious, and mission-critical steps in estate planning is to work with clients to *fund their trusts.* "Trust funding" means changing the title ownership of real estate, the beneficiary designation of policies and annuities, the names of brokerage accounts, and the ownership all other assets, to fit the estate plan. Hours of labor must be invested so that then the plan fulfills the client's goals when a he or she either becomes frail and vulnerable or dies.

A fill-in-the-blank estate plan leads to chaos and an enormous legal fee to do the cleanup work. Many times family members feel cheated and angry by the distribution results of a poor plan.

THE JOINT LIVING TRUST BEAR TRAP

Over the last decade, tax-oriented estate planners have seen the estate tax exemption climb higher and higher. As of 2015, the federal estate tax affects individuals with estates over $5.43 million. It is estimated that this estate tax will affect just one or two of every 1,000 U.S. citizens.

As noted in the previous discussions on funding a trust, all assets must be retitled and/or renamed as belonging to the trust. In the interest of efficiency, cost savings, and simplicity, most couples have been advised to use one joint living trust for their assets rather than the traditional estate-tax-motivated two-living-trust model—one for the husband and one for the wife—in which the estate planner would then "balance" 50 percent of the couple's assets into each trust. A joint trust follows the logic that most couples hold assets in joint tenancy, so a joint trust seems to be an obvious, good option.

Before 2000, I thought a joint trust was an efficient idea, too. But now that I have worked with *hundreds* of couples who come to our office due to long-term disabilities, I know better. Most joint trusts are created as "revocable living trusts." A typical living trust for one person will usually have language that states that if the trustmaker becomes mentally incompetent or dies, then the living trust becomes irrevocable. To become "irrevocable" means that no one can change the trust document.

Now consider the idea that an individual's living trust becomes *unchangeable* when and if the trustmaker becomes mentally incompetent or dies. Then carry this idea over into a joint living trust. Unfortunately, in our fill-in-the-blank world of estate planning forms, there are many joint living trusts that become irrevocable when *only one of the two trustmakers* becomes mentally incompetent. To add to the healthy spouse's woes, the joint trust usually has language that requires that all assets be available for the medical needs of the ill spouse. This language *blocks* the healthy spouse from dividing the trust assets and equitably protecting themselves! They are prevented from using legitimate legal means to avoid excessive impoverishment caused by the spouse's long-term illness.

SWEETHEART WILLS

When thinking about estate plans, most people imagine only a will. The will reads like this: "When I die, I leave everything to my sweetheart. If my sweetheart dies before me, then I leave everything equally to my wonderful children."

In the not-so-olden days, people died quickly. But today, 70 percent of us will suffer from a long and slow decline before our deaths. Your will is totally ineffective until you make the ultimate sacrifice to trigger it—you must die! Sweetheart wills often result in unexpected consequences. When they were created by the two sweethearts, they were probably healthy and vigorous. Long-term care and being in an $8,000-per-month nursing home bed never crossed anyone's mind.

We often recommend changing a sweetheart will to this: "I leave everything to my sweetheart, unless my sweetheart is in a nursing home and has qualified for Medicaid. If my sweetheart is in a Medicaid bed in a nursing home, then bypass my sweetheart and distribute everything equally to our wonderful children."

REVOCABLE LIVING TRUSTS (AKA LIVING TRUSTS) ARE NOT ASSET PROTECTION TRUSTS

As noted in Chapter 5, there are three distinct roles created by a trust document. The ***trustmaker*** is the person who creates the rulebook (trust) that controls the trust assets. The ***trustee*** is the person chosen to manage the assets of the trust according to the rulebook for the benefit of the ***beneficiary***. In the most typical living trust, all three roles are filled by the same person or people. The trustmaker is also the trustee and the beneficiary (during life).

Since the trustmaker controls the terms of the trust rulebook and has total access to all the assets, *creditors* of the trustmaker can reach the assets of the trust. Many people who have living trusts mistakenly believe that their trust creates a "creditor and nursing home cost fortress" around their assets.

Asset protection trusts are sophisticated (expensive) trusts created by highly trained attorneys who concentrate their practice on helping clients who desire these valuable tools. Many of our clients have utilized customized asset protection trusts to avoid excessive impoverishment due to long-term care costs. An extensive knowledge of public benefit law is required to properly design and manage this type of trust planning.

GIFTING CAN BE HAZARDOUS TO YOUR HEALTH

It is said, "It is better to give than receive"; however, you may want to reconsider this old adage in light of the extreme restrictions on gifting that are being placed on seniors under Medicaid laws.

It is no secret that senior citizens are the wealthiest segment of the U.S. population. Much has been written and said about the trillions of dollars that will "change generational hands" as the current seniors pass their wealth to their children and grandchildren. In our line of work, we see many seniors who have used their assets to help out their children and grandchildren. It is not uncommon for seniors to make annual exclusion gifts to their children, contribute to charities, tithe to their churches, and make gifts to their grandchildren for such things as graduation, college tuition, wedding costs, or a down payment on a first home. For some of our clients, this is what the money is for.

We have healthy clients in their 70s or 80s, and they see no problem with helping out family members and making generous gifts. Unfortunately, seniors have to contend with a dirty little secret that was put in place by the prior Republican administration when they passed the Deficit Reduction Act of 2005 (DRA).

The DRA made changes in the way that the government will punish seniors for acts of both charity and giving. The Medicaid rules presume that, when a senior makes a charitable or family gift, the gift was an attempt to get rid of excess assets in order to qualify for Medicaid nursing home expenses. That's right—seniors are guilty until proven innocent. The burden of proof is on the seniors to show that, when they gave money to their church or child, they had some other reason than to qualify for Medicaid.

This DRA rule creates a cruel penalty of ineligibility for Medicaid services if and when a senior who gave away money needs nursing home services at any time within five years after the gift. As long as this law is in place, seniors must remember that the IRS gift tax rule allowing gifting up to $13,000 tax-free is only a tax rule. Giving away $13,000 may cause a senior to suffer a loss in nursing home coverage of two to three months if they need such assistance within 60 months after giving that money away. Thanks to our government, giving may now be hazardous to your health(care)!

MARITAL TRUSTS AND BYPASS PLANNING

Not very long ago, the estate tax was imposed on most middle-class estates. The standard and routine way to reduce or eliminate the estate tax for couples was to create a plan that divided the assets into two "buckets" at the time of the first death. Although there are certainly exceptions to this rule, most of the time the husband dies before the wife.

Another basic fact has been that men accumulated and controlled more assets than their wives. Based on the above realities, attorneys advised the couple that at first death (assumed to be the male), all of the assets with a cumulative value that remained under the estate tax limits would be transferred into a "bucket" called the family trust, or the estate tax exempt trust. The virtue of this trust is that the assets in this trust escape estate tax *both* at the time of the first death (usually Dad) and at the time of the second death (Mom).

Only the excess taxable assets went into the second "bucket," which is called the marital trust. *All* of the assets in the marital trust escaped estate tax at the first death (Dad)—and Mom had full access to all of those assets during her lifetime.

On the other hand, Mom is *not* the only beneficiary of the family trust. It is called a family trust because both Mom and Dad's children are the beneficiaries of that trust. Mom has limited access to the assets in the family trust, and she can be sued by the adult children if they feel that she is not safeguarding their interests.

When the estate tax limit was low, most assets wound up being distributed so that the marital trust received substantial assets, and the family trust received some assets. But look what happened in 2010 to the taxable estate tax threshold: it is now over $5 million per person. Any married couple with less than $10 million will not reach the estate tax threshold.

Now, if Dad dies with $5 million or less in his personal estate *and* with a traditional family trust and marital trust split—all of his assets will be placed in the family trust and *zero* will be placed in the marital trust. Lawyers call this "bypass planning." Mom gets bypassed—and Mom is not going to be happy!

This is another important reason to update your current estate plan.

Zach on the Probate Pothole . . .

Myths, Mistakes, and More

Probate is the legal process of administering the estate of a deceased person by resolving all claims and distributing the assets of the deceased under a valid will. We have already talked about probate a few times in this book. It's an important but often misunderstood process. Here I present two of the main myths people have about probate so you can avoid this pothole at all costs.

Probate Myth Number One: "If I have a will, my estate won't go through probate."

I am not sure how this urban legend came to be. Somewhere along the line, it was likely deduced that if no will means probate, then having a will means no probate. As we discussed previously, this is not the case.

There are actually two paths through probate: one traveled by an "executor" and another traveled by an "administrator."

If you die owning assets in your name alone (and no beneficiaries on the account) that exceed $100,000 and you have no will, your estate will go through probate on the "administrator path." Because you have left no instructions regarding your estate and you have appointed no individual to manage your instructions, the court will appoint an administrator. This person will actually petition the court to be appointed, and then they will pay your bills and divide up your stuff in accordance with the laws of descent and distribution (your closest relatives, or "heirs-at-law"). Depending on the nature of your estate, it could be administered "supervised" or "unsupervised."

If you die with the same assets and you have a will, your estate will still go through probate on the "executor path." It is important to note that *even if you named an executor in your will, that person does not hold the office until appointed by the court.* The executor will then follow the instructions you left in your will regarding who gets what. If your will includes the standard language that your executor may serve without the purchase of a liability insurance policy, that cost can be avoided (unlike the administrator path). Wills can be renounced by a spouse, and they can be contested.

So, the short response to myth number one is this: will or no will, your estate can still go through probate. And why is probate so bad? In short, it's public, it's expensive, it's a major hassle for your family, and it's dangerous for your loved ones and your assets.

On the other hand, the trust could be your hero to allow your assets to pass to your heirs and legatees outside of the probate process and in a private venue. If you have a trust and your assets are titled in that trust, your pour-over will goes on file at the courthouse when the person dies in what is referred to as the "unproven or unprobated" will file—and since it simply states you left everything to your trust, your estate does not go through probate and your plan is private.

When needed, a trust can also be a safe, private way to disinherit individuals, such as children who have financially abused the parents. Additionally, in the case of second marriages, a trust can allow you to keep your assets separate in order to leave them to the children from your first marriage and not to the second husband or wife.

Probate Myth Number Two: "If I have a trust prepared according to my wishes and signed by me, my estate won't go through probate."

A person attends a seminar on trusts, signs up to get a trust, shows up to sign his trust, and then walks away with his trust. What he has is some really nice word processing. He tells everyone he has a trust and he will avoid probate.

He comes in and shows us this trust and tells us that he will avoid probate. We see the lovely, leather-bound notebook. Inside, we see the boilerplate revocable living trust, statutory powers of attorney for healthcare and property (sometimes they are exactly as they appear in the Probate Act in their "form" state with instructions on what should "go here"—the attorney has not bothered to do anything but fill in the name of the principal and agents), and a pour-over will.

At this point, we ask to see the client's current financial statements to see *what is actually in the trust.* Typically there is nothing! Most likely there was some letter written to the client that said in essence, "Here's your trust; put stuff in it." However, the client probably did not read this letter as it was just a part of the lovely leather-bound book, or the client had no idea what "you will now need to fund your trust" even meant.

*Trusts must be **funded** or they do not avoid probate.* If assets are not placed inside the trust, they will be subject to the probate system if the client dies. The pour-over will states that at the individual's death, the trust is the beneficiary. Since the client was not guided through and assisted with the funding process, the assets must first go through probate to be funded into the trust. So whatever they paid to be the proud owners of a trust—no matter how reasonable they thought it was—it was not money well-spent.

***In a funded trust,** your assets bear the name of the trust.* Any real estate is titled into the trust via a deed. Financial accounts are titled, "The John Doe Living Trust dated January 1, 2000, John Doe, Trustee." Assets that cannot be owned in the trust, such as an IRA, can list the trust as a beneficiary. Annuities and life insurance can either be owned by the trust, or the trust can be listed as the beneficiary to make sure that all instructions from the trust apply to this asset.

Don't just do a will; do a trust—and then *make sure your trust is funded* to avoid probate.

TRANSFERRING THE HOME TO ADULT CHILDREN

One common mistake we see is when the home of the senior is transferred to an adult child or children. This occurs sometimes when the parent suddenly becomes ill and the children panic. They transfer the home in an attempt to protect the home from the high cost of healthcare. We hear statements like, "We didn't want the nursing home to take the house." Sometimes it is an attorney who has prepared and recorded the deed transferring the home.

This results in several problems. First, the senior parent is no longer the homeowner, and therefore this may affect the real estate taxes. The senior can lose the senior exemption, the homestead exemption, and even a senior freeze[2] if they have one.

2. The state of Illinois allows a senior who meets the financial criteria to have their real estate taxes "frozen" at the amount in the year the senior freeze takes effect. The senior's real estate taxes will not be affected by increases due to new taxes or a recent assessment. Some seniors elect for a senior tax de-

Of course, this transfer is a huge problem if the family needs to file for Medicaid. If the home is worth $150,000, the senior will be in a penalty period of approximately 24 to 30 months. Finally, if the home is sold, the child could be facing capital gains tax. Even though he/she received the home as a "gift," taxes will have to be paid on any amount over the price that the senior originally paid for the home. In many cases, we are looking at homes that the parent has owned for 50 years and paid about $15,000 for—and now it is worth 10 times that. The children would pay federal and state capital gains taxes on $135,000 in this scenario.

We generally have to "undo" what has been done in haste and without much forethought and little or no knowledge of Medicaid.

UNNECESSARILY HIGH FUNERAL EXPENSES

Very often, people have traditional life insurance policies that they are planning to use to provide funds for their funeral. Some clients will even tell us that they have a small savings account that they have set aside for funeral expenses. Unfortunately, Medicaid does not allow either,

---

ferral. This means that the senior (again meeting a certain financial criteria) can not only have their taxes frozen, but can stop paying the annual tax and allow it to accrue as a lien against the property without the county considering them in arrears and having the taxes be sold at a tax sale. All of the senior tax benefits would be lost if the house is transferred.

unless it is no more than $1,500. The problem with the traditional life insurance is that it has "cash value" and therefore, Medicaid would require that it be cashed in and spent on care. You can, however, have a prepaid funeral plan at a local funeral home or a prepaid burial trust funded by a life insurance policy. The prepaid funeral policy goes to the funeral home at the time of the person's death and is used to cover all final expenses. If a client has a life insurance policy with a large cash value, this can be converted to a burial trust—and the money is now protected for final expenses.

ELDER LAW ESTATE PLANNERS CAN HELP SMOOTH THE ROAD

In light of these potholes, it's time to reiterate the role of the elder law estate planner. The elder law estate planner provides legal advice and counsel to seniors so they can protect their home, their loved ones, and their independence. We counsel clients so that they know the law. Just as a tax attorney advises clients how to arrange their financial affairs to provide the best financial outcome under the law, we do the same as it relates to long-term care. We work within the law to lessen the financial assault of long-term healthcare expenses. We wish to provide a means to help our clients pay for quality healthcare and avoid being in a situation where they have been reduced to having only $2,000 of assets and a personal needs allowance of only $30.

Some of the options that exist under the law include:

- Helping couples with long-term care issues improve the quality of life for both the ill spouse and the well spouse

- Helping couples with long-term care issues plan for improved survivor care financial benefits after the death of the ill spouse

- Assisting the over-65 wartime veteran who may qualify for certain benefits to pay for in-home healthcare assistance and/or assisted living facility costs

- Creating supplemental care trusts designed to pay expenses for frail seniors so they will be able to use their own assets for personal and medical expenses, while at the same time qualifying for Medicaid to pay for their nursing home care

- Providing seniors with appropriate estate planning and trusts designed to fulfill the goal of leaving a legacy to the family

- Assisting senior couples distressed by long-term care issues to improve the well spouse's quality of life both now and after the death of the ill spouse

It is rare for today's senior to have a long-term care insurance policy with sufficient benefits to provide meaningful help with nursing home expenses. Without health insurance benefits, they are forced to pay out-of-pocket for any home health assistance or assisted living facility care.

Today we are faced with the clash of an ever-growing number of people needing long-term care services versus state and federal governments being overwhelmed by the cost of healthcare. In Illinois, because the federal government passed The Deficit Reduction Act of 2005 (DRA), the state is required to release new and more stringent Medicaid regulations. The DRA includes regulations that intensify the nightmare of long-term care. The DRA requires that when seniors use their own money for gifts to family members within five years of the time that those seniors need nursing home care, they are then denied Medicaid payments. The worst part of this law is that the senior will be denied care at the very moment that he or she is most vulnerable.

Once a senior is in need of long-term care, Medicaid will impose penalty rules under the DRA. Any transfer of assets will "hang above them" until the senior applies for nursing home assistance (after having been reduced in assets to less than $2,000). The big question then becomes this: How can a senior pay for care if they have a penalty period of ineligibility after they have already reduced their assets below $2,000? No one really knows for sure, and it is unlikely that the federal government has an easy answer. The DRA was crafted as a punishment for seniors who give their money away to children, churches, or charities. Most seniors have no idea that the federal and state governments intend to deny them long-term care services for doing the things within a family that are designed to support and encourage family life. The DRA also wreaks havoc on the payment streams to nursing home facilities and other providers.

At Law ElderLaw we have a mantra: We never want our clients to be out of money and out of options. While there is an incredible amount of information and risk when it comes to long-term care, we know the honest ways to smooth your road and protect you, your loved ones, and your independence.

Chapter 10

THE ELDER CARE JOURNEY

DEALING WITH DECLINING HEALTH, INCREASING EXPENSES, AND THE NEED FOR MORE MEDICAL CARE

THE ELDER CARE JOURNEY

The "elder care journey" is a continuum of possible care needs that get more intense as the journey progresses. Typically, the journey progresses as follows:

- **Healthy, vigorous senior:** Most of today's seniors are active—much more so than in years gone by. Several decades ago, you were not likely to see seniors playing tennis, running in races, or skydiving! But with today's medical technology and more exercise resources for health-conscious seniors, more people in their sixties, seventies, and even eighties are living full and active lifestyles . . . at least for a while.

- **Medications and acute health problems:** At some point, it is likely that even a healthy and vigorous senior will begin to experience some type of health issues. These issues may start small, with arthritis or high blood pressure. But over time, most seniors will begin to exhibit more signs of physical aging and the onset of more serious issues, possibly resulting in hospitalization for various surgeries or to recover from injuries.

  At this stage in the journey, these issues—and the corresponding medications that are prescribed—will most likely be covered from a cost standpoint either by Medicare (which covers acute care) or private insurance. Although the senior may be responsible for paying an insurance deductible, these costs are often capped at an annual rate, so the senior can plan and anticipate their healthcare financial responsibilities.

  In addition, those who are covered by Medicare may also have a Medicare Supplement Insurance policy that covers many of the copayments and deductibles that Medicare does not cover.

- **Declining senior with memory or mobility issues:** As the senior progresses on the journey, memory and/or mobility will begin to decline. Regardless of how active or healthy one was in the past, at some point the body and the mind will begin to slow down. These issues may start small, such as frequent forgetfulness or walking at a slower pace, until eventually the senior may need some type of in-home assistance to help with basic daily needs.

- **In-home assistance:** When a senior is unable to perform basic ADLs—either physically or because they cognitively are unable to remember to do so—then some form of in-home care is needed. This could entail hiring a homemaker aide to help with household chores or bill paying, or more extensive assistance might be needed on a more regular basis.

Regardless of the need, at an average cost of $17 to $22 per hour (eight hours per day x 365 days per year = $49,000 to $64,000 per year), the expenses can add up.

Now the senior and their family may begin to realize that regular health insurance, as well as Medicare and Medicaid, are not constructed to pay for these types of care costs. In fact, it is often only personal assets or long-term care insurance that will cover these types of expenses. And, unless the senior is suffering from a very serious condition, the situation could go on for years.

- **Assisted living facility:** A time comes when the senior is unable to live at home without assistance throughout the day and night, and it may be unsafe for him or her to attempt to do so. At this time, even though the senior may not need medical or skilled nursing care, the family will need to consider an assisted living facility.

  Here the senior will maintain a great deal of independence while having access to care and assistance whenever needed. Again, *these costs are not covered by Medicare or regular health insurance policies.* Payment for this type of care requires paying out-of-pocket or using long-term care insurance. (In Illinois, we do have "supportive living facilities" that take Medicaid, but you must meet the financial requirements and pass a screening that shows you require a certain level of care. All "assisted" living facilities are not "supportive" living facilities; therefore, Medicaid is not an option in the traditional independent or assisted living facility.)

  With an average monthly cost of $3,000 to $6,000, the annual cost for an assisted living facility is

$36,000 to $72,000 per year. An average length of need is two and a half to three years. Here again, the potential to quickly deplete personal assets is high without some form of pre-planning for this need.

- **The fragile senior at a nursing home:** Once the senior's health deteriorates to a certain level, they will have no choice but to enter a nursing home where they can receive around-the-clock skilled care. Skilled nursing facilities are equipped to handle most conditions, and many even have a special section for patients with Alzheimer's disease.

  The average monthly cost of care in a skilled nursing home facility is $4,000 to $9,000 ($48,000 to $108,000 annually), with an average length of stay two to five years. The only real options for payment coverage are out-of-pocket, Medicaid (only if the senior is considered to be at the state's poverty level), or a long-term care insurance policy.

- **Death:** When the senior has passed away, a whole host of other issues will come into play. This can include survivor care if the senior is leaving behind a spouse, as well as estate administration. Pre-planning in this area is also essential, as the senior's estate could be subject to hefty estate taxes, and his or her heirs could end up with nothing to show for a lifetime of work and saving by the senior.

Rick on Inflation and Lost Purchasing Power . . .

Recent findings in a survey done by the Society of Actuaries (SOA) found that almost 63 percent of older Americans reported that they are not confident that they can save enough to handle the healthcare costs in retirement. In fact, nearly two-thirds of those who were surveyed stated that an annual increase in healthcare costs of only 1 percent to 5 percent could be manageable.

However, findings from the U.S. Department of Health and Human Services has found that healthcare costs are expected to increase, on average, by 6 to 7 percent annually—about 1 to 2 percent ahead of GDP growth—until the year 2019. And that could make health-care costs even more difficult for senior

Americans—enough to affect their ability to maintain their current standard of living in retirement.

In addition to that, cost of living adjustments in Social Security checks have not increased as much as seniors' actual expenses. Healthcare, nursing home, and assisted living costs are just a few of these expenses. Others include daily necessities like food and utilities, which tend to rise faster than the moderate rate of general inflation. This could put many seniors in a financial bind.

Topping things off are market losses in stock accounts, IRAs, and 401(k)s. Seniors who depend on interest payments from their savings are suffering from historically low interest rates.

There's no denying that seniors' purchasing power will decline if they are living on a fixed income—especially in light of the fact that their healthcare costs will rise, and even more so if the need for long-term care arises. On average, once an individual reaches age 65, their chances of needing long-term care at some point are nearly one in two, with the average length of care being two and a half to three years.

If an individual be diagnosed with certain conditions, there is a good chance of an even longer need for care. For example, on average, an individual with Alzheimer's disease could need long-term care for eight years. At an average cost of over $70,000 a year—and rising—it doesn't take long to see that healthcare costs could wipe out even a large investment portfolio in a very short amount of time.

EXPENSES

Seniors who do need long-term care can face enormous expenses that will be detrimental unless properly planned for. And the cost of receiving care, whether that care takes place in a facility or at home, continues to increase each year.

Overall, the nationwide average daily cost for a private room in a skilled nursing facility in 2014 was $240 per day, with the average daily cost of a semi-private room at $212. This equates to approximately $80,000 per year.

But the costs don't stop at that $80,000. For example, when considering a married couple, if one spouse needs care and the other remains at home, the food, shelter, and utility costs don't stop for the spouse living at home. Therefore, this exorbitant cost of long-term care is tacked on to expenses that the couple already has.

More modest forms of care can also take a huge chunk of portfolio assets. The national average monthly base rate for an assisted care living facility in 2014 was $3,500—equaling an annual rate of $42,000.

Even the cost of home healthcare can be daunting. In 2014, the average hourly rate for a home health aide was $20. Depending on how many hours per week they are needed, these costs can add up as well.

When an individual is in need of long-term healthcare, people often turn to their own assets or savings to pay for such care. Unfortunately, due to the high cost of care, it won't take long for assets to be spent down and for funds that were originally earmarked for retirement savings to disappear.

If not properly planned for, the need for long-term healthcare over a period of years can confront a family with three choices of means to pay for it:

- **The family can provide the necessary care informally (if they are able).** However, doing so can come with serious costs to not just finances, but also to emotional and physical health.

- **They can pay for care from an income stream.** This, however, can come at a cost to both lifestyle and ability to meet continuing financial commitments—especially if there is a healthy spouse still responsible for regular household and other living expenses at home.

- **They can pay for it with investments.** If the illness or need for care lasts long enough, there could be a need to liquidate assets, potentially creating tax liabilities and jeopardizing the financial viability of the surviving spouse as well as children who may be depending upon an inheritance.

There are, however, many issues that can affect a person's self-funding options for long-term care. These can include:

- **Market conditions:** Markets go up and markets go down. In a situation where the market drops and an individual or one spouse in a married couple needs care, there could be pressure to sell assets for the liquidity that is needed to pay for the care. However, any loss in income that results from exposure to the decline in the market may render the family unable to pay for both lifestyle needs as well as care. In addition, even if the family does not need to currently invade investment principal to pay for care, they may be compelled to sell assets anyway because they fear that the market may drop even further or fail to recover.

- **Liquidity:** If the individual or family has most of their assets placed in investments that are hard to liquidate, such as real estate or a business, then self-funding the long-term care costs may force them to sell these assets, also at reduced prices.

- **Taxes on the sale of assets:** When individuals sell assets, they are likely to have to pay capital gains taxes on the gain.

- **Lifestyle:** The issue of lifestyle should never be underestimated. The income that is generated from an individual's or a family's portfolio may be able to support their lifestyle, but will it be able to simultaneously support both lifestyle and paying for long-term care?

- **Legacy assets:** Does the family own inherited property that they intend to pass to the next generation? Paying for long-term care out-of-pocket may make this impossible.

In addition to self-insuring out of one's own assets to pay for care, many feel that their family will take care of them when the need for care arises. Yet as much as family and other loved ones intend to care for their elderly relative or friend, it can turn out to be quite difficult when the time comes. Over the past several years, societal changes have made it more difficult for family members to care for a loved one who is in need of long-term care. The economy has forced many families to split up and move apart.

Many families today have both spouses working. If a family member who needs care moves in, more than likely, one of two things must happen: either one spouse must quit working to take care of their loved one or someone must be hired to give the needed assistance while both spouses work. Both situations result in lost income for the family.

Although they should not be relied upon as the sole funding source for long-term care, there are several public financing options available to pay for certain types of long-term care services. There are, however, numerous criteria that a person must meet in order to qualify for financing from these programs. And, even if one qualifies, the benefits received may or may not be sufficient to pay for the entire cost of care that is received.

MEDICARE VERSUS MEDICAID

Although they should not be relied upon to pay for all healthcare and long-term care related expenses, the government offers some assistance for these costs—provided that you qualify. It is important to state upfront that even though the terms Medicare and Medicaid sound similar, *they are very different programs* with differing qualification criteria. When considering the options to pay for care, you must be sure that you understand what each program may or may not cover, as well as what you will need to do in order to qualify for coverage.

WHAT ABOUT MEDICARE?

We went in-depth into Medicare in chapter 4, but here's a brief reminder in context of the elder care journey.

The Medicare program covers Americans age 65 and over, *regardless of their income and their assets*, as well as certain disabled individuals under the age of 65. The Medicare program does not provide medical care directly, but instead it pays doctors and hospitals directly *or* reimburses patients who have paid bills themselves.

Medicare was built on a 1965 acute care (short-term care) model *designed to provide healthcare for the individual who has a probability of recovering from his or her ailment.* It was *not* designed to take on the cost for diagnoses such as Parkinson's disease, Alzheimer's, dementia, or long-term mobility problems. Medicare does not provide care when someone is diagnosed with a long-term chronic condition from which they are not expected to recover.

Medicare does not cover all medical expenses of seniors. For example, it does not cover routine physicals, eye and hearing exams, dental care, self-administered prescription drugs, and many other medical products and services. Many long-term health problems requiring custodial care (care primarily for the purpose of helping with activities of daily living) or private nursing care are also not covered, nor is any care that is not considered to be "reasonable and customary."

Few people realize the limitations of Medicare, and this can wind up costing them a substantial loss of funds, as well as dignity, if or when they get hit with long-term care expenses. Remember this: *Medicare is not designed to pay for long-term care.*

WHEN MEDICARE WILL PAY FOR A NURSING HOME

Nationally, Medicare covers only about 5 percent of all nursing home costs, and the parameters for qualification are many. In the instance that an individual has a condition where they will need short-term care, such as rehab following a surgery or care following an accident, then they may qualify for some skilled nursing facility benefits from Medicare.

Even if a patient qualifies for a Medicare-approved nursing home stay, they are still responsible for paying a daily co-payment of $157.50 between days 21 and 100 (as of 2015). Therefore, they will still need to pay $12,600 out-of-pocket ($157.50 x 80 days). And after day 100, they are responsible for 100 percent of the charges due. It is easy to see that even with some coverage by Medicare, the cost of nursing home care can add up quickly.

Medicare will also pay some of the costs of home healthcare. It will not cover costs for an individual that needs help only with activities of daily living (ADLs); however, Medicare will cover the expenses of medical care in the home, including help with ADLs, if it is part of a doctor's orders.

In order to receive home care coverage from Medicare, the home care agency that is used must be Medicare-approved, and the patient must also meet certain qualifications of their Medicare, Medicare Advantage, or Medicare Supplement plans. To meet the criteria set by Medicare in order to qualify for home care coverage, the patient must need part-time nursing care, physical therapy, speech language therapy, or occupational therapy, and the patient must be homebound. They may also get care in an adult day care program that is Medicare-approved and state-certified.

These services are typically covered by Part A or B of Medicare. The patient will pay $0 for all covered home health visits. If the patient has a Medicare Advantage Plan or a Medicare Supplement policy, they need to contact their plan and ask about their coverage, as they may need to use one of the home care agencies that the plan lists as approved.

Seniors need to remember that Medicare leaves many gaps in coverage by way of coinsurance and deductibles.

Even those who own a Medicare Supplement policy must understand that these policies only offer coverage that is supplemental to what Medicare covers.

If an individual incurs expenses that are not covered in the first place by Medicare, such as non-essential cosmetic surgery, then their Medicare Supplement policy typically won't pay for the coinsurance or deductible. As a general rule, Medicare Supplement policies also do not cover custodial care or long-term nursing home or home healthcare.

For more detailed information on Medicare Plan A, B, and D; Medicare Advantage Plans (Plan C), and Medicare Supplemental Insurance (Medigap), see chapter 4.

MEDICAID

While Medicare is a health insurance program that is an entitlement regardless of an individual's income or assets, Medicaid is not. Medicaid imposes some strict qualification criteria, but in general, it may cover long-term care in a skilled nursing facility when the patient meets certain conditions described in this section.

Medicaid is jointly funded and administered by the federal government through the Centers for Medicare and Medicaid Services and each state. The responsibility for developing the guidelines for the federal/state cost sharing lies with the U.S. Department of Health and Human Services. This department is also responsible for overall supervision of state and provider participation in Medicaid. Each individual state government has fairly wide latitude in running their Medicaid programs.

Even though benefits may be added by individual states at their own option, all states are required to cover the following long-term care-related services:

- Inpatient hospital services (with the exception of services in institutions for tuberculosis or mental diseases)

- Outpatient hospital services and rural health clinic services, including any ambulatory services that are offered by such clinics and otherwise included in the state's Medicaid plan

- Other laboratory and X-ray services

- Transportation to medical facilities

- Physicians' services furnished in the office, the patient's home, hospital, skilled nursing facility, or elsewhere, or medical and surgical services that are furnished by a dentist where state law permits either doctors or dentists to perform such services

- Skilled nursing facility services, including custodial care, but excluding services in institutions for tuberculosis or mental diseases, for individuals age 21 or older

Medicaid is considered to be a means-tested program, meaning that participants must meet strict income and asset criteria in order to qualify. It is considered the safety net for the impoverished. And, in many cases, Medicaid is the "payer of last resort" for skilled nursing facility benefits. It may cover long-term care in a skilled nursing facility when the patient meets two conditions:

- The patient's personal income and asset holdings are under strict limits

- The patient meets medical criteria that are established by his or her state

Medicaid divides individuals' assets into three classes:

- Countable assets (also referred to as non-exempt or available assets in some states)

- Non-countable assets (also called exempt assets)

- Inaccessible assets

Countable assets include any personal financial resources that are owned or controlled by the applicant for Medicaid benefits. These resources must be spent on the patient's care. Countable assets typically include:

- Cash

- Stocks

- Bonds

- All general investments

- All tax-qualified pension plans if the applicant is retired

- Deferred annuities if they are not annuitized

- A primary residence, if the net value of the residence exceeds a cap that is set by the individual state (this rule does not apply if there is a spouse living in the home)

- All life insurance with cash surrender value, if the death benefit exceeds $1,500

- Vacation property

- Investment property

Non-countable assets are acknowledged by Medicaid; however, they are not used in determining eligibility. These assets typically include:

- A small sum of money, called a cash allowance, that is normally under $3,000 (amount differs from state to state)

- A primary residence (if it does not exceed a certain cap amount)

- A prepaid funeral

- Term life insurance

- Business assets (if the applicant derives his or her livelihood from them)

- A car for personal use

- Personal items

Inaccessible assets are resources that would have had to be spent on the Medicaid applicant's care, or, in the case of a primary residence, would have been subject to a lien for recovery of benefits. However, particular assets can be considered inaccessible if they have been transferred to another individual or have been placed in a trust.

Medicaid also has the right to review an individual's financial records at the time that an application for benefits has been received. State Medicaid programs evaluate each applicant's financial situation prior to granting access. They look for transfers of countable assets within certain time periods, referred to as **look-back periods**. For single individuals, Medicaid also considers all assets classified as countable to be spent on skilled nursing home care before eligibility is granted. The individual would be allowed to keep assets that are considered as non-countable.

For married couples, all countable assets are considered as being jointly held and available to be spent on the institutionalized spouse, subject to certain spousal allowance limits. The **spousal impoverishment rule** allows the community spouse (the healthy spouse) to retain a certain amount of assets and income.

Beyond this allowance, all of the couple's assets, earned by and held in the name of either partner or jointly, are generally considered countable and available to fund the institutionalized spouse's care.

The community, or healthy, spouse's assets are considered to be countable even if

- There is a premarital agreement that the assets belong to the community spouse and shall not be claimed by the other
- They were never contributed to by the institutionalized spouse
- The couple lives in a community property state (i.e., where assets that are brought into the marriage are not subject to division in a divorce)

There is, however, an exception to this rule in some states. If the community spouse has a tax-qualified investment plan that currently prohibits access to its assets, it may not be considered as part of the institutionalized spouse's assets.

COMMON MISTAKES MADE BY SENIORS

Despite the hurdles of qualifying for Medicaid, it can be a viable source for paying for long-term care needs if it is planned for correctly. There are, however, some things to keep in mind that can prevent qualification for Medicaid benefits. Some things to be mindful of include:

- **Giving away assets too early.** Individuals shouldn't put their security at risk by putting all of their assets in the hands of their children. Precipitous transfers can cause both difficult tax and Medicaid problems.

- **Ignoring important safe harbors created by Congress.** Certain types of asset transfers are allowed without jeopardizing Medicaid eligibility. These include transfers to disabled children, caretaker children, transfers to certain siblings, transfers into trusts for anyone who is disabled and under age 65, and transfers to a pooled disability trust for any age.

- **Failing to take advantage of protections for the spouse of a nursing home resident.** These protections include purchasing an immediate annuity, petitioning for an increased community spouse resource allowance, and in some cases petitioning for an increased income allowance or refusing to cooperate with the nursing home spouse's Medicaid application.

- **Applying for Medicaid too early.** In some instances this can result in a longer period of ineligibility.

- **Applying for Medicaid too late.** This can mean the loss of many months of eligibility.

- **Confusion about the difference between lifetime liens on property and estate recovery.** There are a number of exceptions to lifetime liens on property, but for estate recovery there is only a deferral for a surviving spouse and a hardship waiver.

- **Not getting expert help.** This is a complicated field that most people deal with only once in their lives. Tens of thousands of dollars could be at stake. It is extremely important that people work with experienced elder law estate planners before trying to navigate through the Medicaid maze themselves.

Rick on Finding a Good Elder Law Estate Planner . . .

Will the Real Elder Law Estate Planner Stand Up?

I just finished looking at a county bar association listing of attorneys who identify themselves as elder law estate planners. Frankly, I was a little disturbed to see that some individuals who are general practitioners lawyers also consider themselves to be elder law estate planners. Drafting simple wills and trusts does not qualify an attorney to be an elder law estate planner. Wills and trusts may be part of the elder law process at times, but there is so much more involved than that! Furthermore, litigating cases that have nothing to do with probate or other issues that touch the elderly does not qualify an attorney to be an elder law estate planner.

When trying to find a real elder law estate planner, it's important to understand how elder law differs from traditional estate planning. Estate planning, at its simplest, is death planning. A traditional estate plan is typically designed to do three things:

- Minimize estate taxes
- Avoid probate court
- Distribute assets from the deceased to the deceased's heirs

Elder law, on the other hand, is death planning plus long-term disability and care planning. The elder law estate planner is dealing not only with your estate plan, but also with life care issues in the event that you or your spouse has long-term healthcare needs during the course of your lifetimes. When there is no long-term care asset preservation planning, it is quite common to see families spend a $2 million net worth estate when both a husband and wife have long-term care needs. This is a key focus of an elder law estate planner.

No one wants to be out of money and out of options before they are out of breath. While it's not possible to guarantee specific results, the elder law estate planner works with clients and families to guide them through the minefield of public benefits, VA benefits, Medicare, Social Security, special needs trusts, powers of attorney, and Medicaid. Our job is to improve the quality of life for our clients, not just plan for a happy post-death asset distribution.

So if you are trying to figure out who is the real elder law estate planner, please ask these questions of the attorney or firm: How many Medicaid applications do you do in a year? How many veterans do you assist with the VA Aid and Attendance benefits per year? How many self-settled pooled trust plans have you done this year?

If you are looking for an elder law estate planner to do any of these things, please use an attorney who can demonstrate that he or she is working in that area every day. The issues are complex, and you deserve to work with someone who is fluent in elder law.

CASE STUDY: THE CARETAKER ADULT CHILD

Abigail Morrison was diagnosed with Alzheimer's at the age of 52. Her family had seen some changes in their mother over the past few years. She was agitated, forgetful, and she sometimes said inappropriate things. They had attributed it to a "midlife crisis."

One day, one of Abigail's sons, Steve, got a call from her former employer in a town 30 miles from where Abigail lived. Abigail had driven that morning to a job where she had not worked for 12 years.

Because Abigail had been a single parent from the time her children were little, Abigail's sons wanted very much to care for their mother who had cared so selflessly for them all their lives. As the Alzheimer's progressed, her other son, Andrew, agreed to have Abigail move in with him, and he and his wife provided supervision and assistance for almost three years.

Because of the advice that we provided them, the family was able to save Abigail's home and several other assets using a type of contract that assigned Andrew and his wife as her caregivers.

When the time was appropriate, the children confidently made the decision to transfer Abigail into a nursing home—without feeling any guilt for relinquishing her care to strangers. Thus, Abigail spent the last six years of her life in a quality nursing home, where she passed away peacefully on a February morning. Upon her death, Andrew said, "I know that before she lost her memory entirely, it meant a great deal to Mom to know that we didn't allow her home to be sold. She died happy that she had never become a burden we couldn't handle, and that she still had an inheritance to leave to us after she was gone."

Zach on Memory and Mobility Issues . . .

As you can tell from our stories and perhaps some you have personally witnessed, the retirement ride can get very rough. Our clients have memory and mobility issues, and some have them sooner rather than later.

We fondly remember our interactions with one couple, who we'll call Sue and Marv, who were in their mid-60s. Retire and travel—that was their plan. After all, they had worked hard, raised two sons, and now it was time to relax and enjoy each other. But this was not to happen as planned: Marv was diagnosed with Alzheimer's at age 64.

We have been there for them with appropriate legal documents, legal advice for their estate and elder law issues, and referrals to healthcare professionals that can assist them. I am happy to tell you that Marv is still at home and actually about the same—but this is rare. He has balance issues and has fallen several times and injured himself.

Sue has had health issues as well. She struggles to be Marv's caregiver *and* to care for herself. Their sons have been a good help; however, one found himself unemployed for a period of time.

Needless to say, this is not the retirement ride Sue and Marv imagined, but we will continue to stand by them as they travel the elder care journey.

A Major Crash: 24/7 Care

Emily and John did not even make it to retirement before they had to switch gears from happy young couple with three sons to a family in crisis. John had begun to show signs of extreme nervousness. People referred to him as being "high strung." Emily knew this was not the man she married in her twenties. Now, at age 35, he was becoming more and more irritable and had even developed what she thought were nervous tics.

After seeing several doctors who prescribed everything from antidepressants to possible shock therapy, it was finally discovered that John had Huntington's disease. This is a hereditary genetic disorder, but John's mother was in her sixties and had no symptoms of the disease. Therefore, John's father had apparently had the illness. John remembered that his father had begun to be very agitated in his thirties and often exhibited moments of rage, but the family attributed this to excessive drinking. When John's father died of a heart attack at 41, no one suspected anything else.

The first time we saw Emily, her first words to us were, "Don't tell me to divorce my husband! Every other attorney I have seen has told me to divorce my husband." John was 46 years old then and had been symptomatic for more than 10 years. His disease had advanced to the point that he needed to be placed in a care facility. The children were 12, 15, and 19—and each of them has a 50-percent chance of having this disease. We worked with Emily to place her husband and moved him sixteen times in five years because of rage issues and some inappropriate behavior that can accompany Huntington's. We did her estate plan, which included special needs trusts for each of her children in the event they have Huntington's. We became her advocate and trusted guide through the Medicaid process and all the facility moves.

"I could never have survived this without you," she told us at John's funeral. The journey can be overwhelming and she truly needed help.

Emily's journey is not over. She is still waiting to see if her children will have this dreaded disease. You can test for the gene, and if you have the gene, you have the disease. However, if you test for the gene and you have it, you will never get insurance. This creates a terrible catch-22 that results in a ticking time bomb for the children of a person with Huntington's disease.

Rick on Wives Caring for Husbands . . .

So much of our practice involves meeting with wives who have become full-time caregivers for their husbands. When a husband develops memory or mobility issues, the wife will sometimes try to cover up for him and hide his decline from the children.

We have spent a great many hours working with World War II veterans and their wives in this way. These are proud men who for many years have been in control of the family and the family finances. They share great stories and photographs with us, some of which they have never really talked about before. These men are trying to hang on to some semblance of control and remember the things in their lives that mattered. They are reviewing their legacy. They have been the breadwinner in the family and the leader in the home. Some of the wives we meet have never driven a car or written a check. They are now in a position that they must "take over," and it is devastating to both husband and wife.

The wives tend to feel that they need to keep their husbands at home and provide the care, even when it is affecting their own health and safety. We try to gently review their options. Sometimes the children are insisting that Mom place Dad in a care facility either because she can no longer lift him when he falls or she can no longer keep him (or herself) safe from the dangers caused by his dementia. One woman said, "You are asking me to put the love of my life in a nursing home!" It was not a real protest, but more a statement summing up how she felt in the midst of her crisis. It's hard to see these strong men frightened and confused about what will happen to them and what will happen to the wife that they loved, married, and made a life with, often for more than half a century.

We understand these challenges, and it is our goal to be there for support and guidance as these clients make major decisions in their elder care journey.

Chapter 11

HOW TO FIND A TRUSTED ADVISOR

TIPS TO IDENTIFY THE TOP 5 PERCENT OF PROFESSIONALS

It has been our observation that in every profession there is an elite core at the top. That elite core usually represents no more than 5 percent of the total profession, so we call them the **Top 5**. The Top 5 know how to "connect the dots" in an extraordinary manner to benefit their clients. In our experience, there are markers that identify an individual who provides the highest and best client services. In addition to being intelligent, they are compulsive life-long learners and teachers. They also possess the rare combination of integrity, initiative, and imagination. They use their gifts for the betterment of others. They are not ashamed to be paid well for doing good. They love others and others love them!

Slightly below the Top 5 is an excellent group of professionals who never stop striving to serve their clients. This group usually represents another 15 percent of their profession, so we call them the **Excellent 15**. These are the doctors, lawyers, architects, financial advisors, and other professionals who tirelessly attend ongoing education and to learn how to apply the ideas of the Top 5.

Below the top groups rests the majority: the **Lazy 60.** This group is the 60 percent who are just okay at their jobs. These individuals do not maliciously intend to harm their clients or their patients, but their advice is just average. It's lukewarm. The Lazy 60 just want to collect their paychecks, go home, grab the remote, and watch the newest episode of reality TV. Unfortunately, the Lazy 60 can do tremendous damage to your net worth and your lifestyle. It has been our experience that most people's professional advisors fit squarely within the Lazy 60.

Every profession has a **Bottom 20**, a group that is a danger to their employers, their clients, and their clients' families. This is the group that operates at a level of incompetence that we would characterize as willful negligence and, many times, just plain fraud.

It's in the Bottom 20 that we find the recent case of a handsome neurosurgeon who operated on a patient's spine seven times and fused more vertebrae each time—just so he could run up the Medicare fees. The Bottom 20 is the home of the financial advisor that we saw "churning" the investment account of an 83-year-old widow. His client did not realize that he was sucking her account dry by constantly buying and selling stocks and earning commissions.

Then there is the divorce attorney who continues to file motions and run back and forth to court until the client's assets are consumed by legal fees. He is "churning" his client, too. Eventually, the client is told that it's time to settle, despite the fact that they have gained nothing by the constant delays in the case.

Unfortunately for most people, it is very difficult to tell the difference between the groups. One of the purposes of our book is to help you learn to see the difference and choose advisors who are in either of the top two groups. We have seen the best, the worst, and the mediocre, and we can recognize the difference. We want to teach you to do that. If this is a red-hot issue for you, read on.

SEVEN SUREFIRE TIPS TO HIRING THE BEST ADVISOR

TIP 1: DON'T DO IT ALONE!

The rules of the game are changing rapidly today. You need trusted guides who focus on solving these types of financial and legal problems. These trusted guides won't be found in the form of your favorite bank teller, nor at the local coffee shop, beauty salon, or golf course.

The greatest protection will be with specialized teams of professionals who have both a qualified elder law attorney and an advisor who concentrates in asset protection.

TIP 2: IF IT SOUNDS TOO GOOD TO BE TRUE, IT PROBABLY IS.

It's a common and scary trend today to hear seniors who have made poor decisions based on "buying into great opportunities." For instance, if a financial salesperson tells you about a 9-percent CD when you know darn well the bank down the road is paying 1.25 percent on CDs, guess what? That's a red flag—a giant, waving red flag.

When you hear something that sounds good and you want to believe it, ask the person this simple question:

"So, what are the strings attached?" If they say "no strings," then you need to turn and run.

There are a lot of great financial products with attractive features. But even the great opportunities out there come with "rules" (aka "strings attached"). You need to know what they are and if they are acceptable to you and in line with your planning goals. Always use and trust your own good judgment and common sense.

TIP 3: BEWARE OF "FREE." THERE IS NO FREE LUNCH.

Marketers use bait-and-switch techniques on retirees constantly. We'll outline a few that we are very wary of. First, let's dissect the free lunch or dinner seminar offer. Obviously, when you get an invitation saying, hey I'll buy you dinner—no worries, nothing is ever sold, your good old common sense should kick in and say, "This person is going to do something to get my money." Red flag. I'm certainly not saying you shouldn't go to seminars to learn, but be careful.

Also be careful of organizations that say they help veterans get benefits for "free." In reality, these are financial salesmen. You can only get help with VA matters from a veteran's service organization (like the VFW), an accredited agent or a certified lawyer. Again, "free" here ends up costing you money.

TIP 4: WATCH OUT FOR LEGAL ADVICE FROM NON-LAWYERS.

We know the value of integrating both trust documentation and specific financial products. However, be very cautious when the purchase of a financial product also entitles you to free legal documents to support the plan. This is where you can be "penny wise and fortune foolish."

Our business model at Law ElderLaw is designed for collaboration among like-minded professionals focused on meeting the goals and objectives of the client. No one professional can wear all of these hats and be good at all of these jobs. A key defense from having your money snatched away is to realize that excellent lawyers cost money; and a packaged offer with legal documentation included (based on the purchase of a product) should be a giant red flag.

TIP 5: BEWARE OF ONLINE RESOURCES.

Information online should be viewed with a very skeptical eye. Today it is not uncommon for retirees to jump online to do "research." The critical question is, are you getting information from a credible source? This can be very difficult to decipher online.

Information overload is another problem. If you enter the keyword "revocable trust" on Google, you'll come up with more than 6 million articles, websites, and "resources" to look at. The problem is, before you finished looking at 6 million online "resources," you would be dead and your family would be burdened by the cost and time delay of probate! (Obviously this would defeat your original planning goal.)

Yes, you need to do research, but on the right thing, finding the right help. Focus your due diligence on finding the right planning team to assist you.

TIP 6: DEMAND PROOF.

There's nothing worse than getting sold a bad idea. Slick talk can be very persuasive, but it may prove financially disastrous. When seeking professional advice, we recommend that you assess just how accomplished your potential advice-giver really is. How that person answers the following questions should give you a good idea of their qualifications and passion for the work:

HAVE YOU EVER BEEN PUBLISHED IN AN INDUSTRY PERIODICAL?

Industry magazines are looking for real experts because they want their readers to get credible and accurate information.

Both you and the publication need someone who doesn't just talk a good game, but someone who really knows his or her stuff.

ARE YOU AN AUTHOR ON THIS SUBJECT?

Professionals who take time to write have a passion for what they do. They've taken time to spell out their planning methods and beliefs. It's not easy writing a book, so when they do, it shows they are dedicated and serious about their profession and proud of what they do. Plus, you'll be able to obtain their book, read it, and then check that the message they published aligns with the advice they give you in person.

HOW OFTEN DO YOU TEACH OTHERS?

The best way to learn something is to teach that subject to others. It can be very intimidating to stand up before a room full of lawyers and/or financial advisors. The audience is filled with experts who can "blow you out of the water" if they feel you are either incorrect or ill prepared. Ask the advisor or lawyer how often they teach their peers.

DO YOU INVEST IN YOUR PROFESSIONAL KNOWLEDGE?

This question is a great way to gauge the prospective advisor's commitment to staying current on new laws, tax code changes, and cutting-edge ideas to help preserve and grow your wealth. The same goes for lawyers. If you have a large IRA, you might be swayed knowing an advisor has trained with Ed Slott, a recognized expert CPA in the area of IRA planning. Likewise, a lawyer who invests thousands of dollars every year to belong to an elite coaching group is certainly educated on the latest and most effective long-term care planning strategies available to preserve and protect their clients' life savings.

WHICH PROFESSIONALS REFER BUSINESS TO YOU?

It's common to ask for references, but this is a loaded proposition. It's not too hard to find three or four people who like an advisor or lawyer and would give them a good reference, even for members of the Lazy 60. Instead of asking for references, ask the professional in question which other professionals—such as other attorneys or other professionals who commonly work with retirees, seniors, and elders—typically refer him or her.

This question is much different. A number of healthcare facilities refer to us because they know we help their patients pay for care and help their families. That certainly means more than just having a friend or client say nice things about us. The professional referral source has zero incentive to give false praise. To them it's all about how well we get the job done. This is a much more credible source of information to assess just how good an advisor or lawyer is at their craft. Again, truly effective planning advice comes from well-organized teams of professionals, which is logical since no one person can be good at all things.

TIP 7: BE SMART AND TRUST YOUR FEELINGS.

Much is revealed when you meet face-to-face. Within moments of meeting face-to-face, you usually can feel in your gut whether you want to continue to be with that person. We believe that every person who walks through our doors needs to be treated as if they are a member of our own family. We invite you to come meet us and see if you feel comfortable and more secure about your future. There's no cost or obligation to become a client after our initial "vision meeting."

Epilogue

KEITH AND DIANE'S STORY

We have told you some pretty sad stories in this book—some tragic. We would like to end with a good story, a story that ends "and they all lived happily ever after."

Keith and Diane came in for planning. They both had just turned 62, and they had been married to each other for 40 years. Diane stayed home until their two children were both in school. She took a part-time job so she could still be available to be the room mother, to be home when the children got home from school, and to attend all her sons' after-school sporting events and other extracurricular activities. Keith had a good job at a local factory, where he had worked his way up from the tool room to management. Diane eventually went to work full-time when the boys were in junior high so that down the road there would be more money for things like college tuition and weddings. The children are grown and doing well. College tuition and weddings are behind Keith and Diane, and they even have a couple granddaughters. It was time for them to think about their retirement ride.

They hoped to cruise through retirement and enjoy this time of their lives traveling, taking the grandchildren to Disney, and comfortably growing old together. They were smart enough to know that they needed help. They had their home, their regular checking and savings, a couple of CDs, and their investment accounts (some qualified and some non-qualified), which had taken quite a hit in 2008, and they didn't want to live in fear of that happening again. They wanted to make sure that they had a plan in place that would provide for their future and leave an inheritance for their children and grandchildren.

They came to us for guidance. We helped them use qualified funds for lifetime income streams that will give them income until both of them have passed away; this is added to their Social Security and their pensions. These safe income accounts will also offer them long-term care if either of them is ever diagnosed with Alzheimer's or another long-term debilitating disease.

Being healthy and vigorous, they both qualified for life insurance with long-term care benefits, and they will be using income from a "safe place" annuity to pay for the premiums. These policies will provide funds to either pay for long-term care, or if they don't need that, a death benefit of $400,000 to their children.

We created estate plans for Keith and Diane, complete with powers of attorney for healthcare and property, pour-over wills, several trusts, probate avoidance, and real peace of mind. We have become their trusted "road-side assistants" for the retirement ride. They have also chosen us as their trusted guide on their future elder care journey.

When Keith is asked, "What's the money for?" he answers, "It is for our retirement. I want to make sure we enjoy our retirement and Diane is provided for if I die first." When Diane is asked the same question, she says, "Well, I would like to travel, enjoy our grandkids, and live out our lives as comfortably as possible, but I also would really like to leave something for the children and grandchildren." Keith and Diane are cruising through retirement. We are grateful that they chose us to help them avoid some of the potholes so they can live happily ever after.

Appendix 1

MICHAEL LEWIS BIO

CONTRIBUTOR TO CHAPTER 4, "MEDICARE: THE DOLLARS AND CENTS"

Michael Lewis has been involved in the Healthcare Industry for 43 years. He began his career with the Blue Cross and Blue Shield System in North Carolina and progressed to the Blue Cross and Blue Shield Association, after which he accepted a management position with Blue Cross and Blue Shield of Southwestern Virginia. Michael then changed direction and accepted a management position with the largest Physician Group Practice in Virginia and held management position with it for 10 years. In 1992 Michael accepted a key management position with Loyola University Medical System in Chicago. His primary responsibilities with Loyola entailed Revenue Management, Managed Care Contract Analysis, and Fraud and Abuse Compliance.

Beginning in 1999 Michael left Loyola and provided consultation for various physician group practices in Chicago suburbs. Beginning in 2000 Michael accepted a management position with the University of Illinois (UIC) College of Medicine, where he held management positions in the Department of Surgery. His last position was Administrator and Clinical Director for the Urology program at UIC, which involved the overall financial and clinical management of the Urology program.

During his 43 years in the healthcare industry, he has gained extensive knowledge of federal healthcare programs encompassing Medicare, Medicaid, and Managed Care systems. He has previously provided presentations on the healthcare systems and their financial impact on patients and physician practices.

Michael retired from UIC in 2013. Since his retirement, he continues to provide presentations and client services in the areas of Medicare benefits and Managed Care programs.

Appendix 2

RICK'S "KEEPERS"

A BIBLIOGRAPHY OF BOOKS ON INVESTING

High Expectations & False Dreams: One Hundred Years of Stock Market History Applied to Retirement Planning by Jim C. Otar. Copyright 2001. Otar & Associates.

How to Make Money in Stocks: Winning System in Good Times or Bad by William J. O'Neil. Copyright 2009. McGraw-Hill.

Investing in One Lesson by Mark Skousen. Copyright 2007. Regnery Publishing Inc.

Main Street Money: How to Outwit, Outsmart & Out Invest the Wall Street Bullies by Mark Matson. Copyright 2012. McGriff Video Productions, LLC.

Modern Security Analysis: Understanding Wall Street Fundamentals by Martin J. Whitman and Fernando Diz. Copyright 2013. Wiley Publishing.

Safe Strategies for Financial Freedom by Steve Sjuggerud. Copyright 2004. McGraw-Hill.

Stock Market Wizards: Interviews with America's Top Stock Traders by Jack D. Schwager. Copyright 2008. Marketplace Books.

The Dividend Rich Investor by Joseph Tigue and Joseph Lisanti. Copyright 1998. McGraw-Hill.

The Four Pillars of Investing: Lessons for Building a Winning Portfolio by William Bernstein. Copyright 2010. McGraw-Hill.

The Millionaire Next Door: The Surprising Secrets of America's Wealthy by Thomas Stanley and William Danko. Copyright 1996. Simon & Schuster/Taylor Trade Publishing.

Trade Your Way to Financial Freedom by Van K. Tharp. Copyright 2006. McGraw-Hill.

Wealth & Wisdom: A Biblical Perspective on Possessions by Jake Barnett. Copyright 1987. NavPress.

ALSO:

The Van Tharp Institute Workshops for Traders and Investors. Website: www.iitm.com.

Appendix 3

PROFESSIONAL MEMBERSHIPS

Illinois State Bar Association

Chicago Bar Association

DuPage County Bar Association

Kane County Bar Association

American Academy of Estate Planning Attorneys

Wealth Counsel

American Academy of Trust, Estate & Elder Law Attorneys

National Academy of Elder Law Attorneys (NAELA)

ElderCounsel

Better Business Bureau

Appendix 4

WHAT CLIENTS AND THEIR FAMILIES SAY ABOUT US

"Law ElderLaw felt like a caring family of professionals who cared about our family and gave us peace of mind." – *Marion A.*

"They served not only my mother, but created a financial environment where she and her family can live a life that is best for her. She will have a better life, for a longer time, thanks to them." – *Don B.*

"All members of the Law ElderLaw team treated each person in our family warmly, with respect and honor. The staff was always patient, and as the process moved forward, it became even more clear that working with this firm was a good decision for our family." – *A.J.B.*

"[We received] immediate replies to e-mails and pleasant communication on the phone. Law ElderLaw is extremely knowledgeable about the public aid system, and a pleasure to deal with." – *Neil C.*

"Each visit to the office was very nice, always on time, as well as professional without seeming aloof. The staff takes nervous feelings away; it has been like seeing a friend you can trust." – *Florence D.*

"We were treated with respect and dignity; more importantly, with empathy. The lawyers we spoke with answered our questions in a highly professional manner, and their composure placed us in a relaxed state. I would wholeheartedly recommend this firm's services. They are client-centered and compassionate." – *John and Mary L.*

"It was as if a burden had been taken off my shoulders. I had such a feeling of relief when I left the office. My trust grew with each experience I had with Law ElderLaw. Do not be afraid; put yourself in their hands and rest assured that everything that can be done, will be done, with care and compassion." – *Jane L.*

"The first 60 minutes that I spent with just one of the LEL staff members was the most productive use of time connected with the care of my mother that I have experienced in the eight years I have been in this challenging role as her caregiver." – *Thomas P.*

"The staff at Law ElderLaw was available and answered any questions I had in a timely fashion. You have given me and my family peace of mind." – *Deborah K.*

"If I had a question or concern, by the end of the day I had a phone call from [a Law ElderLaw employee]. One time she even called me when she was on vacation . . . this is unheard of as far as I know! Caring is so emotionally draining; it's difficult to have a life. I was so relieved to have expert opinions and follow-through with crucial, important matters. By the time my loved one passed away, so much was already done . . . I had such peace of mind that I was able to speak at my husband's funeral." – *Lucille T.*

"I want you to know what a caring group of people you all are. Keep up the wonderful job." – *Karen R.*

"Very polite staff . . . They were willing to listen and help. I could call any time about things I didn't understand. You can use my name anytime!" – *Bob C.*

"Mom felt much more secure knowing she had someone looking out for her best interests over and above my brother and myself. I was so far away, but you were always just a phone call away." – *Jan L.*

"They treated me as if they had known me and my dad for many years. I felt very confident in all their decisions and was almost sad when we were finished that I wouldn't see them anymore." – *Linda G.*

"I have been remiss in writing this letter sooner, but I wished to ensure I articulated my thoughts regarding my family's experience with Law ElderLaw. . . It is with great comfort and trust in you and Law ElderLaw that provides us with comfort and peace. . . As part of the Greatest Generation, my parents wished to ensure the quality of life and care for each other, never anticipating the end of their nest egg . . . they wished to remain independent and with dignity. Your services have helped with that achievement." – *A. Cook*

"How would I describe the working relationship? In one, Great! Everything I needed was delivered and I never had to call twice. If someone asked about your firm, I would say: The only way to go, no doubt. You took a lot of pressure off me." – *Kathleen*

"Excellent! I could not have asked for more. I was very, very impressed." – *Mack*

"Your firm is very professional and very knowledgeable. By far, the best law firm I have ever had any dealings with. I would always recommend this firm." – *Beatrice*

"Very professional-from the first call to the last meeting. Every time I called with questions, everyone found time for me. I would have lost the house, my mom would have lost everything. You made me feel like I was the most important client you had. – *Lori*

"I can't tell you how wonderfully we were treated. This is a very sad situation to deal with and you could not have been nicer and made us feel more welcome. All my mom worked for all her life was not for nothing-you showed us that! I tell people, 'Use them. Don't hesitate.' Thank you seems a very small way to put into words what you have done for our family." – *Jackie P.*

See more testimonials on our website at
www.lawelderlaw.com

Click on "Guiding Seniors," then "What Our Clients Say."

Index

A

- AABD Medicaid assistance, 138
- Abbott Labs, dividends (increase), 45
- ABN. *See* Advance Beneficiary Notice
- ABSs. *See* Asset-based securities
- A/B trust planning, 135
- Accident-related injury (acute impairment), 221
- Accidents, domestic asset protection, 185
- Activities of daily living (ADLs), 60, 219
  - assistance, 272
  - components, 61
  - performing, 259
    - difficulty, 221
    - inability, 67
- Actuarial Reduction, 203
- Acute care
  - illnesses, classification, 53
  - Medicare coverage, 258
- Acute health problems (seniors), 258
- Acute impairments, 221
- ADLs. *See* Activities of daily living
- Adult children, home transfer, 251
- Advance Beneficiary Notice of Noncoverage (ABN), 94–96
  - form, 95
- Advantage Plan (Medicare Part C). *See* Medicare
- Advisors
  - author status, 300
  - bait-and-switch techniques, 297
  - hiring, advice, 296
  - industry periodical, publication status, 299–300

professional knowledge investment, 301
proof, demand, 299–302
search process, 293
strings, attachment, 296–297
teaching frequency, 300
Aging, realities (denials), 223
AIME. *See* Average Indexed Monthly Earnings
Alzheimer's and the Law (Law), 10
Alzheimer's disease, 6, 21, 71
care, provision, 234
diagnosis, 166, 226, 233, 287
costs, 270
impact, 61, 222
impairment, 220
Ambulance services, 92
Ambulatory surgical center charges, 92
Annual offset calculation, penalty, 211
Annual percentage yield (APY), 42
Annuities, 29
contractual investments, 66
fixed annuities, 64
fixed-income annuities, 43
funding, 179
hybrid annuities, 65–66
income-oriented annuity, 67
indexed annuities, 65
investment contracts, 29
LTC rider, 67
selection, 64
Single Premium Immediate Annuity (SPIA), 65–66
types, 64–66
variable annuities, 64–65
Annuity-based long-term care, 61
APTs. *See* Asset protection trusts
APY. *See* Annual percentage yield
Arthritis (physical impairment), 221
Artificial limbs, 92
Asset-based long-term care, 70
Asset-based securities (ABSs), 39
Asset protection, 167. *See also* Domestic asset protection
tools, 169
Asset protection planning
business planning (level 6), 167, 169
inheritance safeguarding/enhancement/protection (level 4), 157
Law Elderlaw pyramid, 147

legacy wealth living trust protection (level 2), 153
lifetime asset protection (level 5), 165
tax/risk reduction strategies (level 3), 156
ugliest mess (level 0), 150
Wills (level 1), 151
Asset protection trusts (APTs), 130, 136
revocable living trusts, contrast, 241
sophistication, 241
Assets
accumulation, 216
classes, 275–276
countable assets, 275, 276
creditor and nursing home cost fortress, creation, 241
distribution, 115, 283
do-it-yourself asset protection, 186–187
earnings, increase (expectations), 200
freezing, 115
inaccessible assets, 276, 278
loss, liability (limitation), 172
non-countable assets (exempt assets), 276, 277
ownership, 246–247
portfolio assets, care costs (impact), 265
post-death asset distribution, 284
post-death distribution, 234
premarital agreement, 279
preservation, 56
release, timing (problem), 280
sale, taxes, 267
sealed box, 137
statements, 22
titling, 248
trap door, creation, 138
window/look-back, 137
withdrawal, 217
Assisted living facility, 260
Attorneys. *See* Powers of attorney
Automatic Data Processing, dividends (increase), 45
Average Indexed Monthly Earnings (AIME), 203

B

Baby boomers, 15–16, 33, 195
program investments, 25
Back-up agents, absence, 126

Banking, certificates of deposit, 19
Bank-insured product, 72
Bank of America, 46
Bankruptcy creditors, impact, 163
Bear market, experience, 216
Beneficiary (beneficiaries), 131–132, 241
    forms, designation, 156
Berko, Malcolm, 46
Blended marriage, 158
Blue Cross Blue Shield, Plan F, 102
Bonds, 31
    average returns, 36–37
    balance, 14
    countable asset, 276
    coupon, 32
    fixed-income bonds, risk (presence), 34
    fixed-interest loan, 31
    fixed-interest rate (coupon rate), 32
    high-yield bonds, 35
    holder, 32
    junk bonds, 19
    lender default, risk, 33
    maturities, variation, 37
    mortgage-backed securities, 39
    principal value fluctuations, causes, 32
    staggering, 43
    Treasury bonds, 40
Bottom 20, 294–295
Bull market, experience, 216
Bump, 29
Business
    asset protection tools (level 6), 169
    deals, failure (domestic asset protection), 185
    debt, domestic asset protection, 185
    loss, avoidance, 186
    planning (level 6), 167, 169
    professionals, referral, 301–302
Buy-sell agreements, 167
Bypass planning, 243, 245

C

Callable bond, redemption, 38
Call provision, 38
Cancer, 21
 diagnosis, 196
Capital gains, exemptions, 180
Capital reserves, 29–30
Cardiac rehab program, 92
Care
 expenses, 215
 receiving, costs (increase), 264–265
 self-insuring, 268
 24/7 care, 287–290
Caregiver
 characteristic, 224
 selection, 69
Caretaker adult child, case study, 285
Caretaker child, payment allowance, 236
Cash (countable asset), 276
Cash allowance (non-countable asset), 277
Caterpillar, cash reserves, 44
Centers for Medicare and Medicaid Services (Medicaid funding), 273
Certificates of deposit (CDs), 19, 41, 296
 investors, 42
 ladder, 42–43
 value, decline, 43
Chemotherapy services/drugs, 92
Children
 blended marriage, 158
 pension-less children, protection, 160
 self-destructive children, protection, 161
 spendthrift children, protection, 161
 trust protection, 139
Chiropractic services, 92
Chronic care illnesses, 54
Chronic diseases, diagnosis, 226
Claimant spouse, government pension, 210–211
Claim Now and Claim Later Strategy, 209
Clark v. Rameker, Bankruptcy Trustee, 142, 162
Clients
 couple status, 5–6
 safety, 8
 simplicity, 9

Clorox, dividends (increase), 45
Coca-Cola
  cash reserves, 44
  dividends, increase, 45
Cognitive impairments, 221
  causes, 222
  definition, 61
  suffering, 222
  supervision, requirement, 60
COLA. *See* Cost of Living Adjustment
Colgate, dividends (increase), 45
Commodities, 50
  exotic commodities, 19
Community Bank of Elmhurst v. Klein, 142, 159
Community property, 279
Consumer Price Index (CPI), 18
  calculation, 40–41
Contraction risk, 39, 40
Corporate bonds, liquidity risk, 38–39
Cosmetic surgery, 93
Cost of Living Adjustment (COLA), 205, 263
  impact, 209
Co-trustees, 131
Countable assets, 176, 275
Couples
  long-term care issues
    assistance, 255
    quality of life improvement, 254
  planning
    example, 104–113
    rules, 206
  status, 5–6
Coupon
  interest, 32
  rate (fixed-interest rate), 32
Courtroom probate, costs/delays (avoidance), 233
CPI. *See* Consumer Price Index
Creditor and nursing home cost fortress, creation, 241
Crummey notice, 183–184
Custodial care, 220

D

Death, 132, 261
  assets, post-death distribution, 234
  intestate death, 115
  notice, publication, 115
  planning, 127–128
  post-death asset distribution, 284
  post-death probate, 150
  pre-planning, 261–262
  quick death cases, 217–218
  testator death, 128, 141
  trustmaker death, 145
Debt load, addition, 39
Deceased, asset distribution, 283
Deemed filing rule, 208
Deferred annuities (countable asset), 276
Deficit Reduction Act of 2005 (DRA), 242–243, 255
Deflation pressures, 17
Delayed Retirement Credit (DRC), 203
Dementia, 21
  diagnosis, 233
  impact, 61, 222
  life-sustaining measures, 124
Descent laws, 247
Diabetes (physical impairment), 221
Diagnosis lottery, 226–227
Diagnostic services, 79
Dignity for client (D4C) trust, 144
Disabled children (protection), trusts (usage), 139
Distribution laws, 247
Diversified portfolio, creation, 14
Dividend-paying stocks, equity investment, 43
DME. *See* Durable medical equipment
Do-it-yourself asset protection, 186–187
Dollar value, 17
Domestic asset protection, 185
Don't Go Broke in a Nursing Home (Quante), 62
Dow Jones, 65
DRA. *See* Deficit Reduction Act of 2005
DRC. *See* Delayed Retirement Credit
Dual qualified deductibles, 54–55
Durable medical equipment (DME), 79, 92
Durable power of attorney, 124–125

E

Eifrig, Jr., David, 50
Elder care journey, 7–8, 257
Elder law estate planners, 7
    impact, 253
    location, 282
    status, 282–284
Elder law options, 254
Elimination period. *See* Long-term care
Emphysema (physical impairment), 221
Equity investment, 43
Equity market, downturn, 45
Estate
    administration, probate process, 245–246
    closure, 115
    documents, representation, 113
    fair share, 159
    guardian, 120
    preservation, 56
Estate planners
    difference, 6
    elder law estate planners, impact, 253
Estate planning
    advice, 114
    attorney understanding, 147–148
    case study, 305–307
    explanation, 7
    lifetime planning consideration, 114
    problems, 215
    realizations, 148
    trusts, usage, 103
Estate plans. *See* Fill-in-the-blank estate plans
    design, 6–7
    goals, 233–234
Estate protection planning (Law Elderlaw pyramid), 147
    business planning (level 6), 167, 169
    inheritance safeguarding/enhancement/protection (level 4), 157
    legacy wealth living trust protection (level 2), 153
    lifetime asset protection (level 5), 165
    tax/risk reduction strategies (level 3), 156
    ugliest mess (level 0), 150
    Wills (level 1), 151
Estate taxes

credit, 117, 118
elimination, 170–171, 233
imposition, 243–244
IRS, impact, 119
limitation, 245
minimization, 233, 283
Excellent 15 (professionals), 294
Excess earnings test, 205
Executors
named executor, nomination, 128
path, 247
payments, 115
status, 127–128
Exempt assets (non-countable assets), 276
Exotic commodities, 19
Expenses, 264
increase, 257
Extension risk, 39, 40

F

Family farm, term (usage), 169
Family Limited Partnership (FLP), 170
disadvantages, 173
Federal Deposit Insurance Corporation (FDIC), 42
Federal estate taxes, 117
Feeding tubes, consideration, 124
File and Suspend Strategy, 208
Fill-in-the-blank estate plans, 237
Financial accounts, 250–251
Financial advisors
income for life, 9
money, return rate, 8
safety, 8
simplicity, 9
Financial ideas, synthesis, 20–21
Fixed annuities, 64
Fixed-income annuities, 43
Fixed-income bonds, risk (presence), 34
Fixed-income debt, 31
Fixed-interest loan, 31
Fixed-interest rate (coupon rate), 32
FLP. *See* Family Limited Partnership
Foreign currencies, 19

401(k)s, 24, 180
market losses, 263
403(b)s, 180
FRA. *See* Full Retirement Age
Full Retirement Age (FRA), 203–207
filing, 210
receiving, 209
Funded plan, prepaid funeral plan, 253
Funded trust, 250
Funding, advice, 179
Funeral expenses, elevation, 252

G

General partners, 172
Get Money Now and Get More Money Later Strategy, 209
Gifting, 215
hazards, 242
powers, usage, 235
Gift tax credit, 118
Gift tax rule, 243
Gold
pricing, movement (absence), 52
promotion, 19
usage, 51
Goldman Sachs, 46
Government agency bonds, liquidity risk, 38–39
Government Pension Offset (GPO), 210
Government pension, receiving, 210–211
Government pensions, 210
GPO. *See* Government Pension Offset
Grantor (trustmaker), 131, 241
Guardian of the person/estate, 120
Guardianship, 122
requirement, 126

H

Health
decline, 257
gifting hazards, 242
issues, experience, 258
needs, funding options, 53

seniors (condition), 257
Healthcare
powerful powers of attorney, 123–124
realizations, 148
supplemental healthcare insurance, cost (reduction), 24
un-reimbursed cost, 70–71
workers, women (domination), 225
Healthcare cost, education costs, maintenance expenses, and support (HEMS) standard, 130, 133, 141
Health Maintenance Organization (HMO), 98
Heart attack (acute impairment), 221
Heart disease (physical impairment), 221
Heirs-at-law, 247
HEMS. *See* Healthcare cost, education costs, maintenance expenses, and support
Hesselbaum, Zach, 8, 10, 11, 167
High Expectations and False Dreams (Otar), 216
Highly active investing, 50
High-return bonds, purchase, 31
High-yield bonds, 35
Holder, 32
Home
in-home assistance, 259
transfer, 251
Home health agency, services, 78
Homestead real estate, 179–180
Hospice care, 78, 87
Hospital
admission, 82
inpatient hospital services, 274
insurance. *See* Medicare.
outpatient hospital services, 274
Household income, example, 192
Husbands, wife care, 290–292
Hybrid annuities, 65–66
Hydration, consideration, 124
Hypertension (physical impairment), 221

I

IACTs. *See* Income and Asset Control Trusts
ILIT. *See* Irrevocable Life Insurance Trust
Illnesses
    expectation, 217
    qualification, actions, 236
Impairments, 220
    acute impairments, 221
    cognitive impairment, 221
    long-term care requirements, 221
    physical impairment, 221
Inaccessible assets, 276, 278
Income. *See* Retirement
    crisis, 13, 14
    income for life, 9
    income-generation plans, 20
    increase, 32
    maximization, 211–212
    payouts, 29
    sources, 24
    stream, 266
        creation, 144
Income and Asset Control Trusts (IACTs), 135
    creation, 133
    living trusts, 132
    spousal bypass, 135
Income-oriented annuity, 67
Indexed annuities, 65
Individual Retirement Account (IRA), 9, 162, 180
    assets, trustee-to-trustee transfer, 75
    example, 162–163
    funds, protection (Supreme Court determination), 163
    Inheritance Protection Trust, 142, 143, 164
    inherited IRA, loss, 142
    IRA-based LTC policy, funding, 74
    market losses, 263
    monies
        Social Security money, contrast, 196
        usage, 73–74
    Trustee/Custodian, status, 74
    usage, 61
Industry periodical, publication, 299–300
Infinite yield, 18–19

Inflation
advice, 262
impact, 36
inflation-weighted negative yield, 34
measurement, 18
protection, 13, 58–59, 205
Inheritance
blow-out, 142–143
safeguarding/enhancement/protection (level 4), 157
trust creation, reasons, 160–161
Inheritance Protection Trust. *See* Individual Retirement Account
In-home assistance, 259
In-home assisted living facility, payment, 71
Inpatient hospital
admission, 84–85
service, 78
services, 274
Insurance companies
capital reserves, 29–30
financial reserves, 30
Intellectual capacity, deterioration/loss, 221–222
Interest
maturity, 37
payments, term (remainder), 32
Interested parties, 126
Interest rates
decrease, 33, 38
increase, 35
long-term interest rates, 34
risk, increase, 37
Intermediate care, 219
Internal Revenue Code (IRC), Section 1035, 62
Internal Revenue Service (IRS)
gift tax rule, 243
Publication 926, 69
Intestate death, 115
Intrabank lending rates, reduction, 34
Investments
contracts, 29
investment property (countable asset), 277
return, 19, 201–202
risk, 13–14
rules, application problem, 13
structured investments, 46
tax-exempt investments, treatment, 30–31

usage, 266
Investor life cycle, 216
IRA. *See* Individual Retirement Account
IRC. *See* Internal Revenue Code
Irrevocable Life Insurance Trust (ILIT), 181
administration, difficulty, 184
planning/creation, 182–183
Irrevocable trusts, 130–132
IRS. *See* Internal Revenue Service

J

John Doe Living Trust, 250–251
Johnson & Johnson, cash reserves, 44
Joint living trust, problems, 238
Joint trust, 239
JP Morgan, 46
Junk bonds, 19
market, risk factors (impact), 35
meaning, understanding, 33
sale, 32

L

Laboratory services, 274
Law, Diana M., 11
Law ElderLaw
estate/asset protection planning pyramid, 147
protection pyramid, 149
service, 5–6
usage, 133
ugliest mess (level 0), 150
Law, Rick L., 10, 11, 62
Lazy 60 (professionals), 294, 301
Leading Lawyer Magazine survey, 10
Legacy assets, 268
Legacy wealth living trust protection (level 2), 153
Legal advisors
income for life, 9
non-lawyer legal advice, avoidance, 298
safety/money return, 8
simplicity, 9
Letters of office, usage, 128

Level 0 (ugliest mess), 150
Level 1 (Wills), 151
Level 2 (legacy wealth living trust protection), 153
Level 3 (tax/risk reduction strategies), 156
Level 4 (inheritance safeguarding/enhancement/protection), 157
Level 5 (lifetime asset protection), 165
Level 6 (business planning), 167, 169
Lewis, Michael, 77
Licensed practical nurse (LPN) care, 219
Life expectancy, 217
  length, 28
  risk, consideration, 217
Life insurance
  cash surrender value (countable asset), 277
  long-term care rider, inclusion, 67
  policy, cash value, 253
  term life insurance (non-countable asset), 277
  usage, feature, 68
Lifestyle, 268
  planning, 27
  protection, 19
    resources, preservation, 234
Life-sustaining measures, 125
Lifetime asset protection (level 5), 165
Lifetime income, creation, 21
Lifetime reserve days, 82
Limited Liability Company (LLC), 176
  defects, 177–178
Limited partner, 172
Liquidity
  impact, 267
  risk, 38–39
Living, probability, 15
Living probate, 150
Living trusts, 136–137
  income and asset control trusts, 132
  revocable living trusts, asset protection trusts (contrast), 241
  two-living-trust model, 239
LLC. *See* Limited Liability Company
Longevity, 211–212
  examination, 199–200
  fitness, 223–224
  market, misunderstanding (relationship), 215
  risk, 27
Long-term care (LTC), 53. *See also* Annuity-based long-term care

- applicant age, 57
- asset-based long-term care, 70
- benefits, 21
  - duration, 60–61
- cost, 72–73
- coverage, dollar amount, 57–58
- elimination period, 59
- expenses, 217
  - money, provision, 226–227
- facility, relocation, 227
- factors, 57–60
- governmental benefit, absence, 227
- impairment requirements, 221
- inflation protection, 58–59
- legacy assets, 268
- levels, 219–220
- lifestyle, 268
- liquidity, 267
- market conditions, 267
- payment, 268
- phrase, defining, 218–219
- planning, 213
- product purchases, IRA monies (usage), 73
- provision, 55
- rider, inclusion, 67
- self-funding options, 267–268
- services, 274
  - necessity, creation, 221
- women, problems, 223

Long-term care (LTC) insurance, 55–57
- benefits/limitations, 56–57
- candidate, selection, 62–63
- policy holder requirements, 60–61
- purchase, 61

Long-term disabilities, impact, 239
Long-term healthcare expenses, financial impact, 253–254
Long-term interest rates, government control, 34
Long-term memory, impairment, 222
Long-term mobility problems, diagnosis costs, 270
Look-back periods, 278
Love and Protection Trust (LPT), 142, 143
Low-yield investments, inflation (impact), 36
LPN. *See* Licensed practical nurse
LPT. *See* Love and Protection Trust
LTC. *See* Long-term care

M

MAGI. *See* Modified adjusted income
Manager risk, 49–50
Marital home, protection, 234
Marital trusts, bypass planning, 243
Market interest rates, depression, 34
Market losses, 263
Markowitz, Harry, 50
Marriages
    advice, 230–231
    blended marriage, 158
    problems, 230–231
    remarriage, 215, 230
    seniors, marriages (legal problems), 228
MBSs. *See* Mortgage-backed securities
McDonald's, dividends (increase), 45
Medicaid, 273
    AABD assistance, 138
    application, timing (problem), 281
    assets, classes, 275–276
    benefits, 235
    funding, 273–274
    means-tested program, 275
    Medicaid-certified nursing home bed, costs, 227
    Medicare, contrast, 269
    nursing home expenses, qualification, 243
    payer of last resort, 275
    penalty rules, DRA (impact), 255–256
Medical care, increase (requirement), 257
Medical charge, Medicare-approved amount (difference), 90
Medical expenses, obligation, 229
Medical facilities, transportation, 274
Medical insurance. *See* Medicare
Medicare, 77
    Advantage Insurance Plan, 54, 97
    Advantage Plan, 85–86, 99
        purchase, 100–101
    beneficiaries, chronic conditions, 226
    coverage, 270
    deductibles, 54–55
    examination, 270
    long-term care provision, 55
    Medicaid, contrast, 269

Medicare-approved amount
medical charge, difference, 90
percentage payment, 92
money, usage, 271
noncoverage, 270–271
Original Medicare, 96–98
out-of-pocket payment, 226
Part A (hospital insurance), 82
benefits, 78–80
coverage, 272
plan of care, 87
Part B (medical insurance), 88
benefits, 79–80
claim, submission, 91
coverage, 93, 272
deductible, 92
modified adjusted income (MAGI), 88–89
out-of-pocket costs, 90
outpatient physical therapy payment, 94
Part C (Advantage Plans), 78, 81, 97
supplement, contrast, 99
Part D (prescription drug coverage), 96
benefits, 79–80
Plan F, 80–81, 102
skilled nursing home coverage, 60
Summary Notice, 96
supplement
Advantage Plan, contrast, 99
issues, 259
Plan F, 80–81, 102
plans (Medigap), overview, 78
Medicare Supplement Insurance, purchase, 54
Medigap, 78
Memory
care, 54
issues, 286, 290
decline, 259
Merrill Lynch, 46
Midlife crisis, 285
Mobility issues, 286, 290
decline, 259
Modified adjusted income (MAGI), 88–89
Money
amount, 22
necessity, 22

return rate, 8
saving, 201
Moody's, 46
Mortgage-backed securities (MBSs), 39
Multiple sclerosis (MS), diagnosis, 233
Muni bonds, liquidity risk, 38–39
Mutual funds
costs, misunderstanding/non-transparency, 47
investment, 47–48
manager risk, 49–50
no-load mutual funds, investment, 49
preferred mutual funds, 49
12B-1 fees, 48

N

Named executor, nomination, 128
NASDAQ, 65
National Credit Union Share Insurance Fund (NCUSIF), 42
No-load mutual funds, investment, 49
Non-countable assets (exempt assets), 276, 277
Noncoverage, Advance Beneficiary Notice (ABN), 94
Non-lawyer legal advice, avoidance, 298
Nursing home
costs, 227, 235
creditor and nursing home cost fortress, creation, 241
Medicare
approval, 271–272
money, usage, 271
resident, spousal protections, 280
seniors, fragility, 261

O

Obama, Barack, 118
Old age pension, enactment, 195–196
Online resources, cautions, 298–299
Original Medicare, 96–98
coverage, 101
supplement, 99
Otar, Jim C., 216
Out-of-pocket payments, 83–84, 226, 260

Outpatient hospital services, 79, 274
Outpatient physical therapy, Medicare Part B payment, 94
Outpatient prescription drug services, 79
Outpatient status, cost, 83

P

Parkinson's disease, 6, 71
    diagnosis, 166, 226, 233
        costs, 270
    impact, 222
Patients
    asset holdings, 275
    medical criteria, 275
    personal income, 275
Payer of last resort (Medicaid), 275
Pension. *See* Straight life pension
    amount. *See* Survivor.
    government pensions, 210
    income
        loss, 23
        percentage, 190–191
    old age pension, enactment, 195–196
    tax-qualified pension plans (countable asset), 276
Pension-less children, protection, 160
Pension Protection Act
    creation, 61
    importance, 62
    rules, 63
PepsiCo, dividends (increase), 45
Personal assets, usage, 260
Personal debt, domestic asset protection, 185
Personal needs allowance, 228
Pet expenses trust (PET), 145
Physical impairment, 221
Physicians
    office visits, 92
    outpatient hospital visits/inpatient visits, 92
    services, 79, 274–275
    surgical procedures, 92
PIA. *See* Primary Insurance Amount
Plan of care, 87
Pneumonia (acute impairment), 221
Policyholders, fund access, 72

Pooled trust, 145
Portfolio assets, care costs (impact), 265
Post-death asset distribution, 284
Post-death probate, 150
Post-hospital admissions, 83
Post-hospital rehabilitative services, 78
    out-of-pocket payment, 83–84
Pour-over will, 249–250
Powers of attorney, 284
    advice, 120–122
    durable power of attorney, 124–125
    powerful powers of attorney, 123, 124
    powerless powers of attorney, 232
    property, 233
    statutory powers of attorney, 249
Preferred mutual funds, 49
Premarital agreement, 279
Premarital legal counseling, 229
Prepaid burial trust, funding, 253
Prepaid funeral (non-countable asset), 277
Prepaid funeral plan, 253
Prepayment risk, 39
Pre-retirement income, Social Security percentage, 198
Prescription drug coverage. *See* Medicare
Primary Insurance Amount (PIA), 203, 208
Primary residence
    countable asset, 276
    non-countable asset, 277
Principal
    safety, 43
    value, 32
        change, 34
Probate
    asset distribution, 115
    avoidance, 249
    concept, 152
    court, avoidance, 283
    courtroom probate, costs/delays (avoidance), 233
    executor actions, 115
    living probate, 150
    petition, filing, 115
    post-death probate, 150
    prevention, wills (relationship), 126
    problems, 245
    process, 115, 245–246

wills, relationship, 246
Probate Act, 249
Procter & Gamble, dividends (increase), 45
Professionals
author status, 300
Bottom 20, 294–295
business referral, 301–302
Excellent 15, 294
face-to-face meeting, 302–303
identification, advice, 293
industry periodicals, publication status, 299–300
knowledge investment, 301
Lazy 60, 294, 301
search, feelings (trust), 302–303
teaching frequency, 300
Top 5, 293–294
Property
powerful powers of attorney, 124
power of attorney, 134
Purchasing power, loss, 262

Q

Qualified funds, 180–181
Qualified trusts, 180–181
Quality of life, improvement, 254
Quante, Don, 62
Quick death cases, 217–218

R

Railroad Retirement Act, 196
Real estate
homestead real estate, 179–180
taxes, impact, 251–252
transfer, 251
Registered nurse (RN) care, 219
Rehabilitative services, post-hospital admissions, 83
Remarriage, 215, 230
Rental properties, renter issues (domestic asset protection), 185
Reserves, 30
Retirees
bond investment, 37

Retirees, generations (existence), 15
Retirement
assets
distribution strategies, 8
withdrawal, 217
decisions, 193
going broke, avoidance, 216–217
income, 189
sufficiency, 144
planning, 27
calculations, 199–200
retirement-qualified funds, 162–163
risks, 73
road maps, 21
Return on investment (ROI), 29
Revocable living trusts (living trusts), 136–137
asset protection trusts, contrast, 241
identification, 129
Revocable trusts, 130–132
Risk
assessment, 156
tolerance, 19
types, 39–40
RN. *See* Registered nurse
ROI. *See* Return on investment
Rural health clinic services, 274

S

Safe harbors, ignoring (problem), 280
Safety deposit box, usage, 127
Schiavo, Terri, 123
Sealed box, asset movement, 137
Securities
face value, 36
Treasury Inflation Protected Securities (TIPS), 40–41
Self-destructive adult children (protection), trusts (usage), 139
Self-destructive children, protection, 161
Self-settled trust, 145
Senility, impact, 61
Seniors
acute health problems, 258
assisted living facility, 260
care, family provision, 266

couples, assistance, 255
death, 261
DRA punishment, 256
estate planning/trusts, 254
expenses, 264
fragility, 261
health, 257
income stream, 266
inflation, impact, 262
in-home assistance, 259
investments, usage, 266
marriage, legal problems, 228
medical expenses, Medicare noncoverage, 270–271
medications, 258
memory/mobility issues, decline, 259
mistakes, 279–281
premarital legal counseling, 229
purchasing power
decline, 263–264
impact, 262
remarriage, 215, 230
Social Security, importance (analysis), 197–198
SEP. *See* Simplified Employee Pension
Short-term memory, impairment, 222
Simple will, 127, 128
Simplified Employee Pension (SEP), 180
Single Premium Immediate Annuity (SPIA), 65–66
Sjuggerud, Steven, 50
Skilled care, 219
Skilled nursing care facility, rehabilitative services (post-hospital admissions), 83
Skilled nursing facility, 85–86
abilities, 261
benefits, 271
long-term care, coverage, 275
patient discharge, 86
post-hospital rehabilitative services, 78
services, 275
Skilled nursing home, Medicare coverage, 60
Slip and falls, domestic asset protection, 185
Slott, Ed, 301
SOA. *See* Society of Actuaries
Social Security, 9, 189
basics, 202
benefits, 18, 195, 206–207

claim, timing, 200
filing, 208
qualification, absence, 88
changes, 195
checks
cost of living adjustments, 263
loss, 23
claim, timing, 202
considerations, 211
disabled adjudication, 143
filing strategies, 208
idea, 189
importance, analysis, 197–198
income, 190
increase, 213
inflation protection, 205
math, 199
money, IRA money (contrast), 196
planning, 211
premium, deduction, 79–80
shuffle, 190
usage, timing, 198–199
withdrawal, penalties, 212–213
Social Security Act, 196
Society of Actuaries (SOA) survey, 262
Special needs trust, 284
creation, 144–145, 236
funding, 236
Spendthrift children, protection, 161
Spouses
spousal benefit, 206
basis, 208
determination, rules, 207
spousal bypass, income and asset control trusts, 135–136
spousal impoverishment rule, 278
spousal-only benefit, claim, 209
surviving spouse, income benefit (increase), 204
work, quitting, 268–269
SSI. *See* Supplemental Security Income
Standard & Poor's, 46
Standard & Poor's 500, 65
dividend payment, 43–44
movement, 50–51
Statutory powers of attorney, 249
Stock market

decline, 46
run-up, 16
Stocks
accounts, market losses, 263
balance, 14
bond-like stock, 44
countable asset, 276
dividend-paying stocks, 44
highly leveraged stocks, 19
Straight life pension, 190
usage, example, 193–194
Stroke, impairments, 220
Structured investments, 46
products, 47
Succession, 167
Successor trustees, 131
Sunset law, 135
Supplemental care trusts, creation, 254
Supplemental coverage, absence, 77–78
Supplemental healthcare insurance, cost (reduction), 23–24
Supplemental Security Income (SSI), 161–162
Surgery
cosmetic surgery, 93
physical surgical procedures, 92
second opinion services, 92
Surviving spouse
financial viability, jeopardy, 266
income benefit, increase, 204
Social Security checks, loss, 227–228
Survivor
benefit, 206
claim, 210
pension
amount, 191
example, 192
Sweetheart wills, 127, 128, 240

T

Taxes
benefits, importance, 175
liabilities, creation, 266
minimization, goal, 116–117
reduction, 167

returns, executor filings, 115
tax-exempt investments, treatment, 30–31
tax-qualified pension plans (countable asset), 276
Taxpayer Relief Act (1997), 117–118
Tax Relief, Unemployment Insurance Reauthorization, and Job Creation Act of 2010 (signing), 118
Tax/risk reduction strategies (level 3), 156
Tender loving care (TLC) trust, 141, 144
Term life insurance (non-countable asset), 277
Terri Schiavo case (1990-2005), 123
Testamentary trust, 136
Testator, death, 128, 141
Third-party special needs trust, 141
TIPS. *See* Treasury Inflation Protected Securities
TLC trust. *See* Tender loving care trust
Top 5 (professionals), 293
Trap door, creation, 138
Treasury bills, 40
Treasury bonds, 40
annual yield, 43–44
Treasury Inflation Protected Securities (TIPS), 40–41
Treasury notes, 40
Trustees, 131, 241
co-trustees, 131
fiduciary duty, 131
successor trustees, 131
Trust for Minors Act, 120
Trustmaker (grantor), 131, 241
asset holding, 132
death, 145
instructions, fiduciary duty, 131
mental incompetence, impact, 239–240
Trusts
basics, 114, 130, 138
creation, reasons, 160–161
differences, 129–130
dignity for client (D4C) trust, 144
funded trust, 250
funding, 238, 250
identification, 132
impact, 139
income and asset control trusts (IACTs), 132
intake form questions, 143
irrevocable trusts, 130–132
joint living trust, problems, 238

joint trust, 239
language, problems, 154–155
legacy wealth living trust protection (level 2), 153
living trust, 132
love and protection trust (LPT), 142
management, 125–126
marital trusts, bypass planning, 243
pet expenses trust (PET), 145
players, 131
pooled trust, 145
preparation, 249
qualified trusts, 180–181
revocable trusts, 130–132
self-settled trust, 145
special needs trust, creation, 144–145
supplemental care trusts, creation, 254
tender loving care (TLC) trust, 141
testamentary trust, 136
third-party special needs trust, 141
usage, 103
12B-1 fees, 48
24/7 care, 287–290

U

Ugliest mess (level 0), 150
Unexpected illness, expectation, 217
Uniform tax rates, government creation, 117
United States, changes, 16

V

Vacation property (countable asset), 277
Variable annuities, 64–65
Variable index annuities, 19
Ventilators, consideration, 124
Veterans Administration
Aid and Attendance, 138
benefits, 284
establishment, 195
Veterans benefits, 7
Vision meeting, 303
Vulnerable children (protection), trusts (usage), 139

Wall Street, structured investments, 46
Walmart, cash reserves, 44
Wealth preservation, 116–117
Wealth protector trusts (WPTs), 136
WEP. *See* Windfall Elimination Provision
Wills
    basics, 114
    death planning, 127–128
    level 1 (pyramid level), 151
    pour-over will, 249
    probate, relationship, 126, 246
    simple will, 127, 128
    sweetheart wills, 127, 128, 240
    usage
        benefits, 116
        disadvantages, 116
    validation, hearing, 115
Windfall Elimination Provision (WEP), 210
    consideration, 211
Women
    annual income (U.S. Census data), 225
    LTC problems, 223
WPTs. *See* Wealth protector trusts

X

X-ray services, 274

Yield. *See* Infinite yield
    payment, 45
Yield to Broker (YTB), 9–10, 29

Z

Zagula, Matt, 22

WA